PASSING RAIN

a memoir
by

Dorene Buckley Graham

From the Camel's Mouth Enterprises, LLC
http://www.dorenegraham.com/camels-mouth-enterprises-llc
/

Cover Design by Elizabeth Graham

ISBN:978-0-9971862-1-5

www.dorenegraham.com

To Jessie,

Thank you for sharing your life with me and making me a better person for having known you. Thank you for letting me be there when you came into this world and when you left it. My love goes with you, wherever you may travel.

ACKNOWLEDGMENTS

During the time I write about in these pages, I was fortunate to not only have the support of my amazing children, Lauren (Liz) Graham and Lindsey Graham, as well as the rest of my family—Theresa Buckley, Marion Buckley Shoults, Carol Anderson, Maureen McRorie, Cliff Buckley and Cathleen Breed—but I was also blessed with many helpful friends. I couldn't begin to list them all here, but I'd like to acknowledge Lezia Gethers, who was a rock as she listened to my daily reports at work, and Barbara Karraker, who offered not only moral support, but added her clinical knowledge as needed. I'd be remiss if I didn't also convey my appreciation to Larry Graham for being there for our children.

I'd also like to thank the published authors of Georgia Romance Writers, or the Georgia Romance Authors Network, who banded together not only to round up donations during the blood drive for my daughter, Jessie, but who also made sure my two younger children lacked for nothing during a time when I couldn't be with them on a daily basis.

And to Tom Simons I offer a special thank you. You gave me the biggest gift of all, time with my daughter. I'm forever grateful.

Dear Reader,

As an experienced author wanting to reestablish my writing career after having taken a deliberate break, I understand the drawbacks in choosing to write a memoir at this point. As you will see in your reading of this, though, I felt directed to write this story. I was literally following a dream.

That said, I hope you will keep in mind the spirit in which this was written. My purpose is to share our story, in the hopes that in some way it may help at least one reader in whatever manner it may possibly help. In no way, whatsoever, do I mean to upset or hurt anyone mentioned in these pages.

The events depicted here are as accurate as my memory and the restrictions of the written word and passage of time could make them. In certain instances, I have changed names of some of the people and places and condensed events to simplify the telling of them. Conversations are not verbatim in most cases, but I have done my best to convey the content and characters of those involved.

In this edit I have corrected Lindsey's pronouns. While at the time of these events we used female pronouns for them, by the time of the 2018 release Lindsey's preferred pronouns were they, them, theirs. They expressed their desire to have this corrected in the final edits, but when I questioned if that was right, since we didn't use those pronouns at the time of these events, they acquiesced and gave me permission to keep the female pronouns. I regret I questioned their request, though, and should have honored it in the first release.

Other than that, what follows is the recounting of two and a half years that irrevocably changed my life. It is my sincerest desire that my sharing of these events will serve to enrich the life of the reader.

Best wishes to all,

Dorene Buckley Graham

Contents

CHAPTER ONE

From the Camel's Mouth

SOMETIMES EVENTS IN OUR LIVES stay with us, the memories ingrained long after they've occurred, especially the ones we most want to forget—the ones that have left us scarred. They echo through our daily routines, like background noise we've learned to ignore. Then the flicker of a thought, a passing comment or a scent drifting on a breeze catapults us back into that moment, and the grief we've suppressed rises, like a river overrunning its banks.

✷ ✷ ✷

I stood in a high place, both a church and a courthouse. Dark masonry covered the walls, while light flowed through stained glass windows in splashes of yellow, pink and blue. Respectful quiet permeated the space.

Before me stood three camels. Their size and the muskiness of their scent drove me back a step. A commotion broke out among the handlers of the one to my right. They spoke in rapid dialog in a language I didn't understand, but their distress was evident nonetheless.

Something was stuck in the camel's mouth. It knelt before me and its mouth opened like a computer-generated image. I hesitated a moment, then reached in with both my hands.

My fingers closed around an abundance of long, slender objects. They slipped as I gathered them and pulled them from the opening. Light fell across my hands, revealing pencils, pens and paintbrushes, too many to count. Again I reached into the camel's mouth, withdrawing a second bundle and then a third.

The load was more than I could comfortably hold. I glanced around for a place to lay my burden. A door stood ajar off to one side.I entered to find court in session, the judge in her raised chair at the front. I glanced around quickly, not wanting to disturb the proceedings. No shelf, counter or cabinet presented itself.

The judge caught my eye and gave an almost imperceptible shake of her head. With that, I understood the bounty from the camel's mouth was mine to keep.

* * *

I awoke on a chair that pulled out into a bed in Northside Hospital's cardiac care unit, one of the best in Atlanta. A small overhead light shone softly in the otherwise dark room. I rose, unsure of the time or even the day.

The constant inhale and exhale of a ventilator filled the air, the sound incessant, following me into restless sleep and back. It was a sound of both hope and despair—hope that the doctors would find a solution, determine a way to get my daughter's lungs functioning again on their own—despair over

2

the pulmonologist's advice to pray. After all, things have to be pretty dire for a doctor to advise prayer.

Even I, with my endless optimism, recognized that.

I moved to the side of the bed located before the large window adjacent to the nurses' station. Still unaccustomed to the feeling of being in a fishbowl, I squeezed my Jessie's hand. My sweet girl, my first-born, unconscious and fragile, so un-Rain-like. Jessie had adopted the name Rain at some point in her early teens when she'd first explored paganism. The name had suited her.

Her newly grown hair spiked in dark contrast to her pale skin. Her hair had been baby-soft as it had grown back after the chemo. I hadn't been able to resist running my hands over the silky strands. Her lashes lay dark against her cheeks. She'd always been fairly translucent, but never like this.

The tube down her throat protruded from one side of her mouth. A feeding tube disappeared into her right nostril. Two more tubes were inserted into her chest. They drained fluid from around her heart and lungs. IVs pumped medicine into her veins, while electrodes, a blood pressure cuff and a pulse oximeter measured her vital signs, displaying them on the monitor above and behind her.

The CCU staff had been solemn that first night she'd coded when at least half a dozen hospital staff, including a close family friend, rushed her to the unit. I'd almost listened to her blustering and turned the car around and not brought her that night. Thank God I'd ignored her protests.

They'd wanted her in intensive care, but no room was available, so she'd ended up here, where the staff was more accustomed to geriatric patients. One male nurse recalled a young man in his twenties a couple of years back. Rain was the youngest patient any of them remembered.

She was nineteen.

Drawing in a deep breath, I straightened beside her, anchoring myself to heaven and grounding to the earth. I meditated on my chakras, aligning and balancing them, as I'd done on more occasions than I could remember. More deep breaths and I called in the angels, hers and mine, asking for their help.

I intend for this healing to be in Jessie's highest good.
I intend to be a clear channel for Reiki.

My chest warmed with love for my daughter. I let it pour from my heart to hers and then I called in the Reiki, invoking the sacred symbols one at a time, three times each, repeating the sequence three times over.

Time stretched and warped around me. At some point I lost count and asked the angels to guide me, continuing by feel. When I finished I remained at her side, drawing in light and love and sending it to her, imagining us both basking in it.

Unbidden, grief welled up inside me and I breathed deeply to quell it. Here she was still with me, but I missed her, missed her laugh, her frank discussions and even her complaining. How long had we been here, in this room where day bled into night, then into day again, with the continual inhale and exhale of the ventilator and occasional hiss of the blood pressure cuff? How long since this new nightmare had begun?

★ ★ ★

Thanksgiving of 2004 found us in Disney World on a rare trip with my extended family. As I walked beside my sister, Cathleen Breed, I scanned our party, counting heads to make sure we hadn't lost anyone. With my mother, six siblings, the spouses who'd joined us, my three kids, one of Jessie's best friends, Cytney Gueory, also known as Pyke, and my nieces and nephews, we made quite an entourage as we moved through the character-lined streets. I finished my counting as Jessie fell into step beside us.

My youngest child, Lindsey, who identifies as nonbinary, scampered in front of us with one of their cousins, laughing. Jessie, ever intolerant of her youngest sibling, glared after them. I shook my head, hoping the two of them would sustain a truce at least until after the holidays.

"Aunt Cathy, feel this." Jessie pressed her aunt's fingers to a spot on her neck.

Worry rippled through me as my sister frowned and asked, "What is it?"

"A lump," I answered for Jess. "We don't know, maybe a swollen lymph node."

"Does it hurt?" my sister asked.

Jessie shook her head. "I can move it."

"I'm taking her to the doctor next week. We couldn't get an appointment before the holiday." Guilt tightened my gut.

Jessie had mentioned the lump before, though I hadn't been able to feel anything when she'd had me check her neck. I'd meant to have it looked at, but somehow I'd gotten sidetracked. I was still adjusting to my divorce and working full time. I had sole physical custody of my three children, homeschooled Rain and my middle daughter, Lauren, evenings and weekends, and was working my way through a four-book contract during every spare moment I could find.

Besides, we'd just found our way back to normal after that first nightmare, after that time with Jessie about which I'm not allowed to write. We'd already come through fire, through a time no child should have to endure. A scene flashed through my mind: Jessie's gaze falling to the pillow and blanket Lauren and I carried, tears streaming down her face as she crumpled to the hospital floor with the realization we hadn't come to take her home.

My chest squeezed at the memory. My heart had broken for her in that moment. I couldn't comprehend anything more of consequence ailing her, not after everything she'd already been through. Of course, none of that excused me from not getting her to a doctor sooner.

Cathy touched Jessie's arm. "I'm sure it'll be fine."

Jessie nodded. "Sure."

I held her gaze. "We'll take care of it, whatever it is. We'll fix it."

She nodded again and touched her neck as her gaze slid away.

⁎ ⁎ ⁎

One doctor's visit and two failed rounds of antibiotics landed us in an examination room with a general surgeon. Jessie's pediatrician had sent us to him to see if he thought she needed to have the lump biopsied.

Biopsy, the word whispered through my consciousness as though my mind could barely acknowledge it.

The surgeon frowned as he pressed his fingers along Jessie's neck. "I feel some swelling, here." He indicated the spot with which we'd become all too familiar. Then he pressed the opposite side of her neck. "And there's some here, too."

Alarm pumped through me. I met Jessie's surprised gaze as she felt the second lump.

"That wasn't there before," she said.

I straightened. "Does this mean it's spreading?"

"It was probably there and she didn't notice. It's smaller than the other side," he said.

Rain shook her head. "It wasn't there."

The doctor smiled. "Your lymph nodes are swollen. This is often a response to infection."

"She's already been on two different antibiotics," I said.

He nodded. "Sometimes these infections are tough. Different infections require different antibiotics. We try the most common ones first, but they don't cover everything."

I exhaled. "So it may not be anything serious."

"I don't think so, but I can't say for sure. I want to send you to an ear, nose and throat specialist. He may be able to tell what the infection is and determine the right antibiotic."

"So, no surgery?" Jessie asked. "No biopsy?"

Again he shook his head. "I don't see any point in it, but we'll see what the ENT doctor says."

* * *

"Mom, hurry." A note of urgency rang through Jessie's voice a week and a half later.

I glanced at the clock on my dash as I pressed my cell phone to my ear. "I'm on my way, honey. I left early. We have plenty of time before your appointment."

"Larry dropped me and asked them to work me in. He has to be someplace."

"What do you mean he dropped you? He isn't with you?" Why would her father leave her? Why hadn't he told me he was taking her early?

We'd kept him apprised of the situation since her first visit with her pediatrician. When Dr. Rosen, the ENT surgeon, asked us to get CT scans before he saw her, we'd been concerned and asked Larry if he wanted to come to the appointment, where we'd no doubt discuss the results of those scans. Since I'd been at work and he'd been closer to the house, it was easier for him to pick her up and meet me at the clinic.

"He's coming back," she said. "He went up to adult medicine to make an appointment."

I tried to stem my anger. Didn't he realize she was nervous—that she needed moral support? "He couldn't have called them?"

"I told him it was okay, Mom. But will you hurry?"

"I am. I'm ten minutes away. If they call you back, just let them know I'm coming."

7

"Okay."

Shortly after, I pulled into the clinic parking garage. My cell phone rang as I got out of the car. Seeing it was Jessie, I answered, "I'm here."

"They called me back," she said, her nervousness evident in her tone.

"I'll find you. Please ask the doctor to wait if he gets to you before I do."

I rushed through the main double doors, and then stopped in the lobby to catch my bearings. A sign directed me up a flight of stairs, then across a landing to the ENT area. I stopped at the privacy line behind another woman, who was checking in for an appointment.

Impatiently, I waited, the minutes dragging by. At last I stepped up to the check-in counter and explained I was there for my daughter, but they'd already called her back.

"Let me see where she is." The woman clicked her mouse and checked her monitor. Her phone rang and I held my breath as she asked the caller to hold.

At last, she sent me through a heavy set of double doors, then down a hall. I had to ask two more nurses before I found Rain in a room off a side hall.

Worry creased her brow as I entered, but I'd made it before the doctor. I wanted to hug her but didn't want her to know how nervous I was, so I took a seat and set my purse on the floor. "Hopefully we'll get some answers today."

She nodded as a knock sounded on the door. A man in a white coat entered, his dark hair combed back in short waves. A sense of competence surrounded him and I immediately felt at ease.

"I'm Dr. Rosen." He extended his hand and I shook it.

"I'm Dorene Graham." I then gestured toward Rain. "This is Jessie."

He took her hand. "It's Jessie, not Jessica?"

"I hate Jessica," she said, almost smiling.

8

He apparently had a calming effect on her, as well. I relaxed a little as we all settled into our seats, Jessie on the examining table, swinging her legs, her heavy mane of hair pulled up into a pony tail.

"I just came from looking at her scans and I don't want to waste any time." Dr. Rosen clasped his hands.

I stared at his knuckles as concern filled me. Another knock sounded at the door and the doctor frowned.

"It's probably her father," I said.

Larry entered, introduced himself, and then took the vacant seat on the other side of Jessie.

Dr. Rosen leaned forward. "As I was saying, I don't like the look of her scans. I'm afraid it might be lymphoma of some kind."

Lymphoma, another word whispering though my mind. My heart pounded. I met Jessie's gaze.

Dr. Rosen continued, "I'd like to send you directly to Emory's Winship Cancer Center. They can do needle biopsies and tell us for sure what we're dealing with. We don't have the same resources they have. Their lab is on the premises. You can have answers immediately."

*Lymphoma...cancer...*the words echoed through my consciousness. Infection sounded so tame in comparison, so much easier to handle.

At last I found my voice. "Of course, whatever we need to do."

"Are you available now?" he asked. "I don't want to waste any time. The sooner we move on this the better. I'd like to call them to see if we can send you straight there."

"Of course," I said. "I can take her. It isn't a problem."

I met Jessie's gaze again and nodded. "Are you good with this, hon?"

She straightened in her seat. "Sure. Let's go."

Dr. Rosen stood. "Let me call them to make sure they're ready for you. I'll send them copies of her scans, as well."

He left and quiet descended on the room. I grabbed my purse and got out my car keys. I drew a deep breath, and then addressed Jessie. "So, we'll finally get some answers."

She pressed her lips together and nodded.

* * *

Two pathologists waited for us as we made our way through Atlanta's late afternoon traffic to Emory's Winship Cancer Center. After calling work to let them know I wouldn't be back that afternoon, I turned on the radio and tried not to think about where we were going or why.

*Biopsy...lymphoma...cancer...pathologists...*they weren't words that should be in an eighteen-year-old's vocabulary.

The two pathologists were women, one brunette and one blonde. The brunette spoke in calm tones, as though not to frighten us. I wanted to tell her it was too late for that.

"We'll numb her neck on each side, so we can insert the needle and take samples from both areas. It may take several tries until we get a good specimen, but we'll run the analysis and tell you what we find before you leave."

She held up a long needle and turned to Jessie. "It'll be a little uncomfortable, but we'll work quickly. Okay?"

Jessie's gaze riveted on the needle. "Do I have a choice?"

The pathologist shrugged. "You always have a choice, but I suggest you let us do the aspirations. If it's something serious, you'll need to start treatment immediately."

"You can squeeze my hand," I offered. Jessie had never liked shots. She'd always squeezed my hand when she got them as a child.

She shook her head. "It's okay. I can do it."

Nearly an hour later, the grimace on Rain's face indicated all wasn't okay, though. I leaned toward her. "It's hurting, hon?"

She blew out a breath. "I can definitely feel it."

"Can't we give her more of the local anesthetic?" I asked as the pathologist again inserted the needle into her neck.

"We're almost done," the woman answered, her attention on the needle. "We want to get as many good samples as we can."

"And you're sure this will tell us something?" I asked. Jessie couldn't be going through all of this without results.

The woman nodded. "I hope so. We're analyzing these in the lab as we go. We just want to make sure we get the best samples, so the tests can be as accurate as possible."

"And if the results don't tell us anything?" I asked.

The blonde shrugged. "Dr. Rosen may want to take a more extensive biopsy to get a bigger sample."

"Okay." The brunette straightened, needle in hand. "I think that should do it. We'll run these last samples. Hold tight and we'll have some answers for you shortly."

They both left and I squeezed Rain's shoulder. "I'm so sorry you had to go through that."

She rolled her head, stretching her neck. "That anesthetic wore off about half an hour ago, but it's okay." She sighed and her gaze softened. "I think I should get some spoiling for this."

"Absolutely." I wanted to give her the world for having this kind of worry, especially after the past ten months. No one deserved this. Though it was a small concession, I offered, "How about dinner out? Your pick."

"Okay," she said, somewhat mollified.

"At least they're done and we'll know something soon."

Her jaw tightened. She didn't respond and we sat in silence until the pathologists returned. The brunette was the first to speak.

"Well, the results weren't as conclusive as we'd like. Sometimes it's hit or miss with needle aspirations. The cells were hard and it was difficult getting the samples."

"One thing we can rule out, though," the blonde said, "is Hodgkin's lymphoma."

"Oh," I said, not quite sure how to respond. Ruling out one horrible option didn't make all the other possibilities any more palatable. "Well, then that's something."

"We'll send the results to Dr. Rosen and he'll let you know how he wants to proceed. He may want to do an open biopsy, but that will be his call." She smiled. "But ruling out Hodgkin's is a good thing."

Somewhat heartened, but still full of questions, we thanked them. Ruling out Hodgkin's might be great, but we still didn't have the answers we needed.

CHAPTER TWO

The World Tilts off Its Axis

More CT SCANS?" RAIN STARED at me later that week, her eyes wide.

"Dr. Rosen wants to do an open biopsy," I said. "He doesn't like the results from Emory and he wants to be sure. He wants new scans in case anything has changed. He wants to remove one of the lumps entirely and send it for analysis, so they can see what it is once and for all."

Jessie made a swiping motion with her hand. "He can have it, but I get something good if they're cutting into me this time."

I smiled. "You've got it. You'll have some real spoiling. You can have dinner *and* a movie."

* * *

Most days flow into each other, one hardly memorable from the last, but January 20, 2005, will always stick with me. The sun shone as Jessie and I headed back to Dr. Rosen's office. She'd had the open biopsy and the surgery had gone well. For once, our spirits had lifted.

We'd talked about the Emory results and decided Dr. Rosen was being overly cautious. After all, the general surgeon who'd sent us to him hadn't been worried and the Emory pathologists hadn't found anything conclusive. I'd had an incredible need to remain positive, to project the best possible outcome.

I'd enveloped us both in a state of denial.

We'd clung to the hope all she needed was the correct antibiotic, convinced ourselves all would be well. The alternative was inconceivable and we couldn't bring ourselves to dwell on it, so we painted a rosy picture. We'd meet with him, he'd tell us exactly what was causing the infection and what Rain had to take to get rid of it. End of story, end of nightmare. She'd move on with her life, and we'd laugh over how nervous we'd gotten over the entire thing.

Jessie smiled as we exited GA 400 and headed down the shaded side road to Dr. Rosen's clinic. A bandage still covered the spot where he'd taken the biopsy. I breathed in the crisp air as I locked the car and we headed toward the glass double doors. Today we'd have answers, and then we could get back to life as we'd known it.

After a fairly long wait, Dr. Rosen entered the small examination room, the same one we'd occupied when he'd sent us scampering to Emory. Again, the sense of competency radiated from him and I relaxed a little in my chair, even threw Jessie a reassuring smile.

He perched on the edge of his seat, leaning forward, his fingers steepled. "I'm sorry to have kept you waiting. The original results weren't clear and the sample had to be sent for more extensive testing. We just got back those results and that's what kept me."

Neither Rain nor I spoke. I remained focused on Dr. Rosen as he continued, "I'm afraid I was right, it *is* lymphoma, Hodgkin's lymphoma."

I blinked. His lips had formed the words, but he couldn't have said what it sounded like he'd said. Jessie had recently suffered more than any soul should suffer in a lifetime. She already faced an ongoing battle. What Greater Being would now grant her something this unthinkable?

It couldn't be.

"Wait," I said, holding up my hands as though I could push back his diagnosis. "Emory told us specifically it wasn't Hodgkin's."

He shook his head. "Needle biopsies aren't always reliable. Maybe we should have gone with the full biopsy from the start, but I was hoping to save time."

"But how can this be?" My pulse thrummed in my ears. My mind whirled. I forced myself to remain focused on him. I had to take this in. I had to remain calm.

"When you see cancer like this, the cells replicate in a certain way. Hodgkin's presents in a specific pattern. They evidently didn't have a large enough sample at Emory."

I clenched my fists. "It could be a mistake."

Again, he shook his head. "I'm so sorry. I wanted to be sure. That's why I did the open biopsy. That's why we sent it out twice for analysis."

Jessie sat, silent, unmoving. I inhaled slowly. "So, we treat it."

"Yes." He shifted in his seat. "I'm referring her to an oncologist. Call him today to schedule an appointment. You'll want to get her started immediately." He stood. "I'll get the referral ready and have the nurse give you his contact information."

Jessie remained silent after he left, though her gaze spoke volumes. Feeling every kind of inept, I moved beside her. "Oh, honey, it's going to be okay. We'll figure this out. I'm in this with you, you know."

"I know." She nodded, her brow creased, her eyes troubled.

Silence pressed around us and I couldn't bear it. I wanted to scream. "How do you feel?"

Her gaze met mine and for a moment she looked so lost. "I feel like I've just been told I have cancer."

* * *

We ran away that day, unprepared to face the world as it had altered, horrendously tipped off-center. I called work and told one of my three bosses I wouldn't be back that afternoon. She was, of course, very understanding, though it would be the following day before I shared the diagnosis with her. No way was I leaving Jessie on her own to deal with this. Not that day, when the news was raw and overwhelming.

I hung up and turned to Jess. When she'd been younger and gotten hurt, a simple distraction had always worked wonders. "We have the whole afternoon. We can head home if you'd like, or we can do whatever you want."

She thought for a moment. "Fridays. And I want dessert."

"Anything."

"And a movie."

"Perfect," I said. We both loved movies, surround sound, bigger than life characters and a couple of hours to escape—to not think.

We checked the theater first, since it was on the way to the restaurant. We arrived just in time for whatever movie she picked. I think it was "The Adventures of Shark Boy and Lava Girl." I don't really remember and have little recollection of actually watching the movie. I sat in the dark beside Jessie, pretending I was engrossed, while I cried as inconspicuously as possible. Shark Boy and Lava Girl didn't exactly inspire tears and the last thing I wanted was for Jessie to see my distress.

I could only imagine what she felt.

Afterwards, we settled at a cozy table at Fridays. We'd just placed our order—-appetizers, entrees and dessert for Jessie to be brought out first—when we discovered we hadn't quite escaped the world.

"Dorene?"

Surprised, I glanced up. An acquaintance I hadn't seen in some time sat at a nearby table. She waved and smiled, saying, "It's so good to see you. How are you?"

I've never understood why that's a rhetorical question. I've never been great with small talk. I have always felt compelled to answer and to answer honestly. I glanced at Jess, then turned to my friend and forced a smile.

"We're fine," I said, the words falling flat, the lie weighing on me. Not that I cared about answering that particular question untruthfully. I hated, absolutely hated, that we were so far from fine, I was reeling from it.

That would be the first of many instances where I'd stumble over the answer to that question. The lie whirled in my head.

We're fine. We're fine. We're fine.

Hours passed before we headed toward home. I'd called, of course, to check on Lauren and Lindsey and let them know we'd be home later, but I wanted to deliver our news in person. This wasn't the kind of thing they should hear over the phone and the thought of facing them with this had me dragging my feet. Unfortunately, as we'd left the clinic I'd called first Larry and then my sister Maureen McRorie, who lived in Orlando and operated a glass art shop with her husband. Before the holidays, in the face of the ongoing conflict between Jessie and Lindsey she'd asked, "Why don't you let Jessie come stay with us for a while? We'll work school into her helping at the shop."

To say Jessie and Lindsey didn't get along was a gross understatement. Their constant fighting took a toll on all of us. With the added stress, the ever-present tension between them had been escalating of late and we'd all needed a break from it. Until recently, Jessie hadn't had much interaction with my sister since she'd moved to Orlando and this would give them a good opportunity to become better reacquainted. I'd agreed to the trip and we'd planned for Rain to leave within the week.

To be honest, I'd needed to share Jessie's diagnosis with someone who'd understand my devastation. Maureen had never had children of her own, but though she hadn't had much contact with my children since her departure for Orlando, she loved them, and the need to share this new burden pressed me to call my sister. I'd explained Jessie wouldn't be coming for her visit and told her why.

I turned on my phone as we left the restaurant and found a message from Lauren, or Newt, as Maureen had dubbed her when she was very small. Lauren later adopted the use of her middle name, Elizabeth, or Liz, when she enrolled at Georgia State, but to me she was always Lauren or Newt. I listened to the message. She knew and I hadn't been the one to tell her. Disappointment filled me. She should have heard it from us.

Anger at myself for assuming Larry and Maureen would have the foresight to not tell her bubbled inside me. I should have known better than to speak to anyone before talking to Lauren and Lindsey, or at least asked the others not to say anything yet.

I called the house phone and Newt answered, repeating the questions she'd asked in her voice mail. "Mom, is it true? Does Jessie have cancer?"

I hesitated, as though not confirming it made it less real. "Yes. I'm sorry; I didn't think they'd tell you. I wanted you to hear it from us and not over the phone."

"It's okay," she said. "I haven't said anything to Lindsey."

"Thank you, honey. We'll be there in a few minutes and we'll tell you everything we know."

As I hung up, all the energy drained from my body. I drew a deep breath and silently rallied. We'd get through this. Though younger than Jessie, Lauren was mature beyond her fifteen years.

Ten months ago, when Jessie had suffered her earlier illness, I'd sat on my bed that early April morning, in shock over the previous night's events, unable even to choose an outfit to wear to the hospital to visit Jessie. Lauren had come into my room.

I shook my head. "I don't know what to wear."

She went to my closet, removed a dress, and then laid it on the bed beside me. "Wear this, Mom. It looks nice on you."

In that moment, Lauren had stepped into adulthood, taking her place beside me. Looking back, I'm sometimes sorry I accepted her in that role. I feel I cheated her of the rest of her childhood by doing so. I don't know how I would have made it through that time without her, though, especially since Lindsey had been traumatized by the events leading to Rain's hospitalization in the spring of 2004 and I'd had my hands full with dealing with the two of them. Lauren had been fundamental in getting us through the nightmare we'd faced then.

She'd be onboard for whatever was needed in the challenges ahead.

⁂

I felt better once I got online and researched. I didn't have to force my enthusiasm when I told Jessie, "Hodgkin's has a ninety percent survival rate."

Her eyebrows arched. "That doesn't seem so bad."

"Ninety percent?" I smiled, relief flowing through me. "I'll take those odds. People recover from this cancer daily. You'll get through this."

I resumed my positive outlook. I had a profound belief in the creative power of thought and intent, and I visualized Jessie as healthy and strong in every spare moment of my day. At one point, I actually told a friend this was preferable to our last trauma with Rain. This may have been a statement on the emotional toll her last illness had taken; her diagnosis, after all, had been a lifetime sentence.

But this time I felt we faced only a temporary setback. She'd get treatment; she'd be okay. We'd learn whatever lessons we were supposed to learn from this and life would resume as we'd known it.

Now, for an open-minded girl who worked with Reiki, you'd think I'd steer Jessie toward more holistic, alternative treatments. Certainly, a huge part of me yearned to do so. Unfortunately, chemotherapy is detrimental to many alternative therapies and can't be done simultaneously.

And when a doctor tells you your child has cancer that's a frightening thing. My advice to Jessie had been that we'd try the chemo first, before focusing on things like oxygen therapy, Essiac and cesium. We'd go the alternative route if needed, but only after we gave the conventional treatment a chance to work. I wasn't taking any chances with Jessie's health. A ninety percent survival rate certainly seemed promising, after all.

*　*　*

"So, are you two sisters?" The dark-haired woman behind the counter peered at us, her gaze swinging from Jessie back to me.

We'd heard this numerous times before and Jessie always smiled. I think she liked that people thought she looked old enough to be my sister. She shook her head with a wide grin. "This is my mom."

The woman's gaze fell on me. "You're her mom?"

I pursed my lips. Here we were, meeting with an oncologist, an oncologist, for Christ's sake. Did we have to dwell on idle chitchat? "Yes, I'm her mother. She has a three o'clock with Dr. Nelson."

The woman nodded. "You look like sisters. I never would have believed it."

I pulled out my wallet. A number of people had lined up behind us. People filled nearly every seat in the waiting area, a few bald headed, an older woman with a scarf covering her head, a tattooed guy working a crossword puzzle in the corner. My stomach clenched at the thought that they were all here for the same reason. They all had cancer.

Like Rain.

"How much is the copay?" I asked the woman as she continued to shake her head and smile. Who the hell cared if Jessie and I looked like sisters?

She sighed, took my copay and checked us in. "Please have a seat and they'll call her back shortly."

We maneuvered through the maze of seats to two vacant ones along a back wall. I breathed and kept my gaze down. I didn't want to know these people, didn't want to catch glimpses of their stories in the snippets of conversation murmured here and there. I wanted to get my daughter her treatment, get her well and then get us the hell out of there.

"Aren't you going to write?" Jessie nodded toward the book bag I'd set on the floor beside my chair, the one with my AlphaSmart, the little keyboard with memory I used to draft my fun, sexy romance novels.

I glanced at the bag. I had a trilogy due out that fall. I had the second book to edit and the third to write. The deadline for that one loomed.

I shook my head, my stomach tight. "Not right now."

She gestured toward the bag. "Then can I read it?"

She'd already retrieved and read pages I'd thrown into the recycling. It warmed my heart that she read my books and was so supportive. Once, when she'd been around ten, she'd slipped on some rocks while we'd been river walking, and she'd gashed her leg badly enough I'd taken her to urgent care to see if she needed stitches.

She'd watched over my shoulder as I'd filled out the insurance form and when I came to the blank asking for my occupation, she'd said, "Put writer, Mom."

I'd glanced up at her and chuckled. I'd been a stay-at-home mom at the time and though I'd been writing, I hadn't yet sold my first book and we had no indication at that time that I ever would. I was touched that in spite of that fact, she considered me a writer.

She slipped out of the seat beside me and did a little dance with her hurt leg bound with a strip I'd torn from my shirt, singing, "My mom's a writer. She's a writer."

I'd smiled, my heart brimming, and written writer in the blank. I loved, absolutely loved that she was proud of my writing, even if my books, once I'd published, weren't great literary works.

But that day in the oncology waiting room, my enthusiasm was sadly lacking. Again, I shook my head. How was I ever going to write this book? Romance was the farthest thing from my mind at that point.

"Wait until it's released to read it," I said. "By then it'll have gone through all the edits and will be changed so much you wouldn't recognize it."

"That's okay. Let me see what you have so far. I want to read your original version."

I sighed. I did need to write, or I'd never make this deadline. But how was I to write light-hearted romance at a time like this? Finishing it seemed almost meaningless in light of what Jessie now faced.

I pulled out Alphie. "I'll write. You can read the copy edits for book two when we get home. I didn't bring them."

Jessie leaned toward me as I opened the first file and started to type. I stopped and turned to her. "You're not reading over my shoulder while I write. I can't work like that."

"But I want to read the rest of the story."

"Jessica Graham," a woman in scrubs called from a door beside the reception area.

My heart squeezed as I shoved Alphie back in my bag. Rain was the first to the door, her mouth tweaked in that way that said she was annoyed. I smiled at the woman. "She prefers Jessie."

The woman nodded. "Okay, right back this way."

She led us to a small office, crowded with a desk and bookshelves. We seated ourselves on one side of the desk. My pulse thrummed in my ears.

"Dr. Nelson will be with you shortly," the woman said, before leaving.

Silence fell over us. I closed my eyes. Sitting in the oncologist's office, it was impossible not to think about why we were there. God, I hoped Jessie liked him. I'd taken her to more doctors and alternative practitioners in her life than I could remember and she rarely liked any of them.

"You're not going to write?" she asked.

"No, not now."

Her gaze held mine for a moment, and then she nodded. I drew a deep breath and pulled a notebook and pen from my bag. "Did you think of any other questions you want to ask?"

She stared straight ahead. "No."

I opened the notebook to the page of questions I'd written and reviewed with her earlier. It included notes I'd taken while I researched Hodgkin's. I reread the same question several times over, unable to focus on its content.

The door opened in due time and a man I assumed was Dr. Nelson entered, white coat flapping, his thinning hair combed neatly over the top of his head. He introduced himself, and then sat behind his desk, leaning back, his hands folded over his rounded belly.

He told us about Hodgkin's, confirming much of what I'd already learned. He talked about drugs with names too long to pronounce, so they were referred to by acronym.

"We'll schedule her for six cycles of the ABVD regimen. We'll get CT scans periodically to monitor the chemo's progress in shrinking the masses in her neck and chest," he said. "I believe you've already scheduled with the surgeon to get her portacath?"

"Yes, she'll see him next week."

Since our appointment with Dr. Rosen, Jessie had endured two more CT scans, blood work, a pulmonary function test, a bone scan, and gallium and mugga scans. And all this we'd worked around my full-time job and our home schooling. We hadn't been able to schedule her surgery sooner.

He nodded. "Good, she'll be able to start chemo then. We'll also want to do a bone marrow biopsy before we get started. If you're agreeable, I'll have Janice check the schedule to see how quickly we can do that and if we can work her in for chemo as soon as she has her portacath."

We talked more about the portacath, a device the surgeon would implant in her arm through which she'd receive the chemo, because, evidently, without it the toxicity of the chemo could scar her veins to the point they'd be unusable. We also further discussed the bone marrow biopsy and what it would entail.

Dr. Nelson explained, "We need a sample of the marrow to see if the cancer has spread there. It's the only real way to see how pervasive it is." He paused briefly before asking, "Any more questions?"

I shook my head. I'd already gone through my list, diligently noting his responses. My mind was on overload, sorting through all we'd discussed, all we had to do to get her through this. "No more from me. Jess?"

She shook her head.

The doctor nodded. "So, shall we ask Janice to come in to get everything scheduled?"

I looked to Jessie. We'd discussed pursuing conventional treatment before trying alternative methods, but at eighteen she was old enough to decide her own fate.

"You're in the driver's seat here. It's your call, hon," I said.

She chewed the inside of her lip, and then nodded. "Let's do it."

CHAPTER THREE

Our New Normal

THEY'RE GOING TO DRILL INTO MY pelvic bone?" The fear in Jessie's voice squeezed my heart.

"They need to make sure the cancer hasn't spread into your bone marrow. We talked about the biopsy with Dr. Nelson."

"I didn't know they were taking it from my pelvic bone."

"I'm sorry, honey, I'll stay with you, if you want."

Her gaze met mine and my heart further constricted. She should be hanging out with her friends, not sitting here dreading a bone marrow biopsy. I tried for a reassuring smile.

"They give you a local anesthetic to numb the area."

"Can't they knock me out?" she asked.

"I don't know, but I'll ask them."

She frowned. "Okay."

When the nurse called her a short while later, I headed back with her, but the nurse stopped me at the door. "You aren't allowed in the room during the procedure."

All my mom instincts rebelled. "Even if she wants me there?"

"I'm sorry. It's policy. It will be easier if you wait out here."

Easier for whom? "Well, can they give her something stronger than the local anesthetic? Can they sedate her?"

The woman touched my arm. "She'll be fine. We do this procedure all the time."

I glanced at Jessie, feeling completely incompetent. "I'm sorry, honey."

She nodded, her jaw firm as she followed the nurse through the door. I took my seat and pulled out Alphie. I'm not sure how many times I checked my phone for the time or glanced at the door, but after what seemed an eternity the nurse finally called me back.

She smiled. "All done. She was a little tense, but we got the sample. She did fine. Dr. Nelson will call you with the results when he has them. You can see her now."

I followed her down the hall and around a corner to the examination room where, though dressed, Jessie lay on her stomach, her face hidden in the crook of her arm. The nurse left me with her, and she rose up onto her elbows. Moisture brimmed in her eyes and a telltale red colored her nose. As tough as Rain was, I'd never seen her appear this shaken.

I touched her arm. "Are you okay?"

"It hurt, Mom. I tried not to, but I screamed."

My throat tightened. A mixture of anger and sorrow flooded me. I hated this. "I'm so sorry, Jess."

We'd learned long ago Jessie got mean on caffeine, so she didn't get to enjoy it much, since she could be plenty mean all on her own, as Lauren and Lindsey could attest. But this seemed a time to make an exception.

I drew a deep breath and tried for a light tone. "Well, I think you get a Mountain Dew® for this one."

A grudging smile curved her lips. "A big one."

"Whatever size you want, hon."

"And I want you to read to me."

"You've got it."

* * *

I stared at the flashing cursor on my monitor the following day. Two weeks. I had just over two weeks to finish this book. I'd stretched the truth a little by telling others I was one-hundred pages in, but I wasn't quite that far into it.

My stomach was in knots. I took the fact that I'd signed this four-book contract for a stand-alone book and then a trilogy very seriously. This was the final book of that contract, but it had been all I could do to hold things together over the past months.

I'd kept up with my grueling schedule of being a single parent, working full time, homeschooling Jessie and Lauren, dealing with Jessie's illness and writing in the little spare moments I could find, often into the wee hours of the night, and then making do on too little sleep. I'd gotten through the copy edits for book two of the trilogy, but I'd hardly written a word on book three since the proposal had been approved.

I sighed and placed my fingertips on the keyboard, trying to focus on the story at hand. My throat burned and the screen before me blurred as a vision of Jessie teary-eyed on the examining table after the bone marrow biopsy assailed me.

It hurt, Mom. I tried not to, but I screamed.

How was I to do this? How was I to put aside everything that was going on—everything Rain was suffering—to write a romance novel?

I dropped my hands into my lap. Exhaustion claimed me. I couldn't. I just couldn't do it. Somehow I had to explain to my editor that we needed to pull the trilogy. Maybe I could finish this last book later, after Jessie was through this mess and then we'd release all three books at that time. But for now, I just didn't see how I could manage it.

After taking a deep breath, I called Harlequin's Toronto office. This wouldn't be an easy conversation, but the sooner I let them know, the better. Hopefully, they'd find other books to fill the spots. It was an awful thing for me to do, but these were dire times. I'd been very dependable in the past, bringing my first two books in early, when holes had opened in the schedule, and the last one on time. Surely my editor would understand.

She did, of course. Wanda Ottewell and I had been babies together in the book industry, she a brand new editor and I a brand new author when Harlequin bought my first book in September of 2001. We worked well together and I had a lot of respect for her, not just as an editor, but as a human being.

"I can't imagine what you're going through," she said.

The grief and fear swelled inside me. "It isn't anything I'd ever wish on anyone. I just...I'm so sorry. I know it means pulling all three books, but things are...really hard. I wouldn't do a good job right now. I can't write fun and sexy. I don't think I have it in me."

"I really appreciate what you're going through," she said, her tone soothing. "And I support whatever you feel you need to do, but you shouldn't doubt your abilities. You can do this. It's true these books are different from what they started as, but that's okay. You're not the same person you were when we contracted this trilogy, so the books will be understandably different."

We talked for some time, eventually turning to the logistics of scheduling line edits and final edits and somehow, in the end she convinced me. And she was right. I finished that book in a record three weeks, even during the upheaval of our lives. Wanda pulled her strings and worked the schedule to give me as much time as she could, editing in the final moments before the book went into production.

To this day, I'm grateful for her support and encouragement, but when I completed that contract, I needed normal—my kids needed normal, or at least as close to normal as we could manage under the new circumstances of our lives. With the divorce and my going back to work for the first time in seventeen years and all the juggling of our busy schedule, we hadn't had normal even before Jessie had gotten sick. Now, with that to deal with on top of everything else, I couldn't handle another book contract. Not now. And not in the foreseeable future.

Other than the promotional work I'd do on the trilogy, I put all new writing projects on hold. Instead, in the days ahead, I took to my journal.

* * *

For the next several months, our lives revolved around chemotherapy, blood work and CT scans. We were either recovering from a treatment or getting ready for one. On treatment days I sat with Rain in the big chemo room, lined with reclining chairs filled with cancer patients plugged up to bags of chemo. We talked, read and did school as much as she was up to it. I hated that the huge room was always full, never an empty seat.

Since we were still home schooling, Lauren was home to look after Jessie when she didn't feel well and, though I now supported only one boss and he allowed me to work from home as much as I needed, I was able to go to the office most days. At that time, a private owner was buying the company where I worked, one that managed and maintained long-term care facilities throughout the country. Gloom blanketed the office as coworkers whispered to one another about possible layoffs.

"Are you safe?" was a common question asked in the elevator and whispered around the break room.

I didn't worry about losing my job as an executive assistant. I couldn't waste the energy. I had to believe we'd be okay. I didn't have seniority. If I lost my day job, I'd find another, or pick up my writing again and hopefully contract more books. If need be, I'd find a way to get by on child support and the equity in my house until we got through this. Either way, it didn't matter. Worrying about it wouldn't change whatever outcome awaited me.

My focus remained at home, where I breathed a sigh of relief as I pulled into the garage one evening. Music and laughter floated to me from the kitchen and I made my way there, stopping in the doorway.

Jessie sat on a barstool, surrounded by her best friend, Phoenix, his girlfriend, Christine, and Newt. Phoenix ran his hand over the lump in Rain's left arm, on the inside above her elbow. A scar marked where the surgeon had inserted the portacath.

"So, did it hurt?" he asked.

"He put my arm to sleep, but I could feel it. Not pain, but the pressure of him cutting into me, and then digging around inside when he inserted it. It was so gross. It totally freaked me out."

While they talked, Lauren wrapped a ponytail holder around a section of Jessie's hair. Jessie's hair had always been her crowning glory. The day she'd been born, it reached down the nape of her neck in strands so thick the little knit cap the nurse put on her head kept popping off.

After repeated attempts to keep it in place had failed, I had removed it and said, "I don't think her head will get cold."

She'd worn a French braid by the time she was eighteen months old. I'd always loved her hair, even when she'd tried every color and cut imaginable. It was thick and waved with the perfect amount of body.

31

Before she started the chemo, she'd decided if she had to wear a wig, she'd have one made out of her own hair. I'd called and e-mailed every wig making place I could find, but hadn't found anyone who'd agree to make a wig of her hair. So Newt had gone online, found directions on how to make a wig, and then asked me if she could order the supplies she needed. I'd heartily agreed.

Phoenix bounced to the music, while Christine smiled and raised a pair of scissors to one of the sections Newt had tied off all around Rain's head. Distress rose in me. I stepped into the room.

"Wait," I said. "It's so soon. Honey, you still have so much hair."

Jessie shook her head. "It's coming out, Mom, in clumps. I want to salvage all I can."

Lauren handed me a map she'd made of her sister's head. She'd marked areas with letters corresponding to tags she was attaching to the sections of hair. "I'll reattach them in the same order."

I pressed my hand to my chest as Christine made the first cut. Jessie stared at the bundle of hair as Newt tagged it, and then put it in a box. "Make sure you're cutting as close to my scalp as you can."

"I get to buzz it when they're done," Phoenix said.

He wore one small braid in his dark curls, along one side of his face. Before she'd started the chemo, Rain had that same side braid. When I'd seen it on Jessie, I'd thought of it more as an Indian princess braid, but she'd said it was her commander braid, or something like that, saying either the Greek or Roman commanders, I can't remember which, wore such a braid when they went into battle. Phoenix had promised to keep his for her when she could no longer wear hers.

"You want to cut one?" Christine offered him the scissors.

I swallowed as he grinned and snipped a lock. The music swelled and they all smiled. Lauren set out tortilla chips and Jessie's favorite spinach and artichoke dip.

Warmth filled my chest and the room blurred. They were having a hair-cutting party. They were cutting Jessie's hair because she had cancer and was losing it, but people who loved her and who could actually make such an event fun surrounded her.

We were blessed to have this kind of support and Jessie was fortunate to have a sister who would not only learn to make a wig for her, but who would carry out the tedious task.

Still, my throat tightened as I turned from the scene. I'd find Lindsey and give them a big hug. Lord knew I needed one.

I found them in their room, writing in a notebook.

"Hi, Mom."

I scooped them into a hug, and they wrapped their arms around my neck and squeezed.

"I love you," they said.

"I love you, too, honey. How was school today?"

"It was fine." They sat beside me on the bed. "I had a dream last night."

I straightened. They'd had a difficult time when Jessie had gotten so sick before. Nightmares had been a substantial worry. "Was it a bad dream?"

Their eyebrows furrowed. "You'll think so, but I wasn't upset. I felt okay. And I know Jessie and I don't get along, but it wasn't about that."

"Honey, what was it?"

"I was outside and I realized I was standing on a grave." Their gaze met mine. "It was Jessie's grave, Mom."

I pulled them to my side. "It was just a dream, sweetie. Jessie's going to be okay. She's doing well with her chemo. She isn't going to die."

Lindsey pushed away to look at me. "No, Mom, it was real, like I was seeing what's going to happen. Jessie's going to die, but she'll be okay."

A chill ran up my spine. Normally, I held a lot of stock in dreams, but surely we couldn't take this one so literally. Again, my denial kicked in. "Honey, it was just a dream."

"I know you don't want to believe it, but it felt real."

I squeezed their hand. "I believe it felt real to you, but it was a dream. It's understandable you'd be worried and you'd have a dream like that, but we're doing everything to help Jessie. We haven't even begun trying the alternative treatments. If the chemo doesn't work for some reason, she still has lots of options. And Aunt Marion is reviewing books on alternative therapies for us. We're not going to give up."

They held my gaze for a long moment before nodding. "I know. It was a dream. I just wanted to tell you about it."

"Thank you, honey. If you're worried, you can sleep with me tonight."

They picked up their notebook and pencil. "I'll be okay."

I kissed the top of their head. "That's right. We'll all be okay."

* * *

Jessie grimaced as she shifted in the passenger's seat a week or so later. "Can you go any faster?"

"Honey, I know you're hurting, but we'll be early for your appointment as is." I exited the interstate and glanced at my directions to her chiropractor's new clinic.

"Maybe he can start earlier."

Once again, we were on the way to see another doctor. This doctor was different, though. Dr. Rafkin was a chiropractor who also did energy work. I'd first brought Jessie to him a couple of years before to get his opinion on some surgery that had been advised for her misaligned jaw. I'd gotten second, third and fourth opinions from varying orthodontic surgeons all of whom suggested cutting out and repositioning either her top or bottom jaw. I shouldn't have been surprised they'd all advised surgery. They were surgeons, after all.

I couldn't accept the options they presented, though, so had sought the advice of a couple of chiropractors instead. Dr. Rafkin had been the second chiropractor we saw and Jessie had actually liked him.

He was a gentle man, and he'd agreed with the first chiropractor's diagnosis of a twisting of her spine that started in her pelvic bones and spiraled up to her skull, attributed possibly to a fall in her childhood. He'd been treating her over the past year for that and for the accompanying back pain, which sometimes reached intolerable levels. Now, he also used his energy work to lessen the effects of the chemo.

Twenty minutes later, Rain lay on her stomach on Dr. Rafkin's table. As usual, I sat in a chair to the side. Soft music wafted through the room as he circled her slowly, balancing and strengthening her energy as needed. No matter what state she was in before she saw him, she always felt better afterwards.

"How is your pain level now?" he asked her as she rolled to her back.

She nodded. "Better."

He frowned as he moved his hands over her, starting at her head and sweeping downward. He stopped at her throat. "You're having issues with your throat chakra."

My gaze fell to his hands as I sorted through the functions of the fifth chakra and the possible side effects of the chemo.

He cocked his head as he studied her. At some point in his youth he'd begun seeing peoples' auras. He often diagnosed issues by actually perceiving the damage in his patients' energetic fields. What did he see now?

Slowly, he shifted lower, over her heart, and nodded. "There seems to be an issue with her lungs."

"Damage from the chemo?" I asked.

Jessie pushed up onto her elbows. "What kind of an issue?"

"I'm not sure. Relax and let me see what I can do," he said.

Her lungs. I bit the inside of my lip as Dr. Rafkin worked on her. My father had suffered from tuberculosis and emphysema. The emphysema and pneumonia took him when Newt had been an infant. I'd call Dr. Nelson first thing in the morning and ask him to check Jessie's lungs. Maybe we could alter her chemo if needed.

Dr. Rafkin shook his head. "The chemo is very hard on her."

Guilt filled me. "I know, but we thought we'd try it first, before we moved on to alternative treatments."

"And is it working?" he asked.

I inhaled. "Her scans have shown progress. It seems to be."

He frowned, shaking his head as he focused again on Jessie. He didn't say more, but I felt his question hanging over us, unspoken.

At what price?

CHAPTER FOUR

Labors of Love

W E MAINTAINED AS MUCH NORMALCY as we could. Though I faced the imminent layoffs at work, I spoiled Jessie at every opportunity. If she mentioned a book, I bought it for her. If she wanted to see a movie, I took her. If she craved food from a certain restaurant, we ate there. If she'd had a tough day, had been poked, prodded or stuck more than usual, I let her have Mountain Dew.

I'd, of course, asked Dr. Nelson about her lungs, but the pulmonary function tests he ran showed minimal damage, which he assured us would likely be temporary. At one point in the spring, after she'd completed her third cycle of the ABVD, he announced, "Her scans are still showing improvement."

When we reached the house I smiled at Jess. "Let's celebrate by ordering in food and watching a movie."

She nodded but didn't smile. "Okay."

I maintained my positive outlook. "See, no problem, you'll kick this thing."

"But if I don't—"

"Honey—"

"No, Mom, listen. If I don't, then I was thinking I want a Viking burial."

I stared at her. How in the world would I possibly plan such a thing? "I don't think—"

"You know, with archers with flaming arrows."

A shiver of dread ran through me. Why was she thinking along these lines? Why now, when her scans had shown she was beating the cancer?

"I'm not going to talk about that with you," I said. "We're celebrating. Let's not put anything out there like that. No funeral or burial talk. Focus your energy on the positive. Now, where do you want to order food from?"

She shook her head, but my distraction worked as she planned our celebration. I relaxed as she rattled off possible options. At least I'd gotten her thinking in terms of celebrating. I couldn't let her dwell on even the possibility of planning for her funeral.

* * *

We made it to summer and, as always for that time of year, everything in the yard grew like wild. I put my hair up in a ponytail and slathered on sunscreen one Saturday and set to work on the weeds that had cropped up all over. A light breeze fought back the Georgia heat.

The front door opened and Jessie emerged, pale and blinking into the sunlight. Dark crescents hung below her eyes. A paisley scarf covered her head. She settled on the bottom porch step and pulled a handful of weeds from the flower bed beside it. Cicadas whirred all around us.

"Honey, you should be resting," I said. She was wearing a chemo pump that she kept on 24/7. The motor whirred softly. The treatment was tough on her.

She shook her head. "I want to help."

"I've got this. Have you gotten any sleep?"

"I can't sleep." She reached for another batch of weeds.

I settled beside her. "Want me to come inside and read to you?"

She gave me a little half smile. Rain loved to be read to almost as much as she loved to read. She shook her head. "It's okay. Maybe later."

She gestured to the yard. "You shouldn't have to do this by yourself."

My gaze swung from the yard to the house. Since Jessie hadn't been able to go, Lindsey was in Orlando visiting my sister and Newt was catching up on schoolwork because we'd fallen a little behind. The previous year, Jessie had been the one to take on the bushes, clippers in hand. Since my dad had taught us that girls did inside work and boys did outside work, my yard maintenance skills left much to be desired, as my Roswell neighbors could attest. I greatly appreciated Jessie's efforts on that front, but not on this day.

I shook my head. "I don't mind. I don't want you to wear yourself out."

She didn't respond for a minute, and then she touched her neck. "It's back."

My pulse quickened. "The lump?"

She nodded. "It's been there awhile, but I didn't want to say anything." She shrugged. "I didn't really want to believe it. I thought maybe it would go away again, but it's gotten bigger."

I squeezed her hand. "I'll call Dr. Nelson. We'll try a different drug. I'm sure there's a protocol for this."

She drew a deep breath. "I *am* tired. Maybe you could read me to sleep."

My throat burned and I blinked moisture from my eyes. "I'd love to, honey."

* * *

Before we could make it back in to see Dr. Nelson, Jessie spiked a fever and was admitted to Northside Hospital. In addition to the fever, her back pain returned with a vengeance.

"I'll call Tabby and Anna to let them know you're here," I said as I set Jessie's overnight bag in the closet.

Tabby and Anna were a little older than Jessie and when she'd been sick before, they'd been by her side as she'd healed and reemerged into her social circle. They'd want to be there for her now.

"No."

"Honey, they'll want to know you're in the hospital."

"No," Jessie repeated, her voice stern. "I don't want you to call anyone. I don't want them worrying about me."

I didn't answer right away.

"I'm serious. I don't want you to call anyone."

I sighed. "Okay, I won't, but I still think they should know."

Jessie glared at me.

"I won't. I'll respect your wishes." I got that she didn't want her friends worrying about her, but it would be nice for her to have the additional support.

She closed her eyes and grimaced as she arched against the headboard of the hospital bed. "It's pounding down my spine."

"I'm so sorry, honey." My frustration swelled. How many times through this process had I uttered this useless comment?

The pain in her back had intensified since her admission into the hospital. Several inquiries of the staff elicited merely the shrugging of shoulders.

40

"She shouldn't be having that pain," one of the nurses said.

"But she is," I said.

"I'll talk to the doctor about increasing her pain medication."

"But we need to figure out what's causing her pain. Masking the symptoms isn't going to help."

"But she shouldn't be having back pain."

I stared at the nurse's retreating back, then at the pain etched across my daughter's face. That awful helpless feeling engulfed me. Something was terribly off here. What were we all missing?

"Mom, it really hurts."

"I know, honey. I'm so sorry." *Lame. Lame. Lame.*

"Will you Reiki me?"

I scooted forward. "Of course I will."

Thankfully, her pain eventually abated and her temperature returned to normal. We were able to bring her home after just one night, though her hospital stay only left me with more questions.

* * *

"It really hurts." Jessie cradled her left arm, the one with the portacath. She'd been out of the hospital for only a matter of days when this new pain had assailed her.

Dr. Nelson frowned. "We'll do an ultrasound. It's likely you're having some clotting issues with the portacath."

"Clotting?" I asked. Didn't we already have enough to deal with?

He nodded. "We'll have to start her on a blood thinner, after she sees Dr. Rosen again. I'm sure once he sees her latest scans, he'll want to do another open biopsy and we can't have her on a blood thinner for that. Have you scheduled with him?"

"Yes," I said. "He does want to do another open biopsy on the latest lump. She's scheduled for surgery next week."

"Good. We should move on this right away," he said.

* * *

The landline rang as I entered the house through the garage. I caught it on the third ring. "Hello?"

"Mrs. Graham, this is Dr. Nelson. I've spoken with Dr. Rosen about the results of the latest open biopsy he did on Jessica."

It had been almost three weeks since Jessie had told me the lump had returned. I pressed the handset to my ear and sank into the old rocker by the door. "Yes, Dr. Nelson?"

"Well, as you know, the swelling has returned to her neck. The scans showed an increase in the masses in her neck and chest, and the biopsy confirms she's relapsed."

Relapsed? How could she relapse if she'd not yet recovered?

He continued, "The masses show significant growth. I'm referring her to Dr. Bradford at the North Georgia Blood and Marrow Transplant Group. They specialize in bone marrow and stem cell transplants."

I nodded, though he couldn't see, but I couldn't form a coherent response. I scrambled for a notepad and pen. Blood pounded in my ears. *Bone marrow transplant? Stem cell what?*

"So, she needs a bone marrow transplant?" I asked.

"I'm recommending a stem cell transplant, but you'll consult with Dr. Bradford and decide."

"What exactly is that?" I stared at the note pad where I'd scribbled the words. "There isn't a different chemo she can try?"

"In the case of a relapse of this sort, the normal response is a stem cell transplant. There are other drugs, but they're more likely to be less effective than the ABVD regimen in which she's already failed."

She failed? My blood heated. She hadn't failed. The damn chemo had failed her. "So, this stem cell transplant...do you mean...embryonic?"

"The stem cells we'd transplant are her blood stem cells. The idea is to use a high-dose chemo that will hopefully kill all of the cancer at once. Unfortunately, this kind of chemo can have a detrimental effect on the blood cells, as well. Dr. Bradford's group would collect the stem cells to keep them from harm's way during the high-dose chemo. Then they return them later and the stem cells grow into whatever blood cells she needs."

Again I nodded, though numbness blanketed my mind. "So, you think this transplant will help her? You think her chances are better with this treatment?"

He paused, as though choosing his words. "This is the next step I'm recommending in her treatment. I don't see any other alternatives."

* * *

"It's finished." Lauren held up the wig she'd painstakingly made from her sister's hair.

"I can't believe you sewed in each one of those," I said, lifting a handful of the strands.

"Let me see it." Jessie grinned in anticipation as she took the wig.

"Well, it got a little stretched out of shape." A frown marred Newt's expression as Jessie tugged on the wig.

I'd helped Lauren cut the base fabric into which she'd sewn the hair. We'd done our best to mimic Rain's hairline. Jessie moved in front of the entryway mirror and we all gathered around to see her with her new do.

"What the..." she yanked on the wig, twisting it one way and then another.

I pressed my lips together to suppress a laugh. The hair stuck out in wild disarray. "Maybe if we tried to style it."

"I don't think we can," Newt said. "It's too fragile. It's okay if you don't want to wear it."

"No offense, Lauren, I know you worked hard on this, but it looks like hell." Jessie pulled the wig from her head. "I think I'd rather be bald."

I took the wig from Rain and slipped it on, this time unable to hold in my laughter. "It looks like road kill."

Lauren shrugged. "Now we know why no one would make a wig out of her own hair. Maybe she dyed it one time too many. It is a little dried out."

After laying the wig aside I turned to her. "But what a labor of love."

"Yeah," Jessie said. "I really appreciate that you tried."

"I'm sorry it didn't work out."

I turned to Jessie. "Honey, I'm happy to buy you a wig."

She nodded slowly. "And meanwhile, Newt can henna my head."

"Sure." Lauren beamed at the prospect.

Among other things, Lauren was quite the artist. What a fun way for her to display her talents.

* * *

Lauren did a beautiful job with the henna, drawing an intricate design on Jessie's head. I glanced at Jessie the following week and smiled as we drove to the wig shop. She'd left her scarves and hats at home and displayed her sister's artwork with pride.

"There's the shop." Jessie pointed to the wig store beside a little metaphysical shop in the small strip shopping center.

"I see it."

44

A woman sweeping the walkway in front of the metaphysical store glanced up as we approached. She smiled and waved toward Jessie's head. "Girl, I love it. You are beautiful."

"Thanks, my sister did the henna," Jessie said, smiling.

"Let me see." She gestured for Jessie to turn around as she reviewed the intricate henna design. "That is gorgeous. And you do the bald thing really well. I have a girlfriend who chose to go bald. She just decided one day she didn't want to deal with her hair anymore and she shaved it all off. She looks amazing. Not everyone can pull it off, you know. But she could and you do, too. You have a nice shape to your head."

"Thanks."

"That takes courage. I really commend you."

"Thanks," Jessie repeated as she stroked a hand over her head and glanced at me.

I smiled. In spite of her location beside a wig shop, it didn't seem to have occurred to the woman this hadn't been a matter of choice. With Jessie beaming under her praise, my preference would have been to hug the woman rather than tell her we were on our way to buy a wig, especially since Jess wasn't inclined to mention it.

The woman's praise had a lasting impact. Though we bought a wig that day, Jessie never wore it out anywhere. In fact, when I asked her about it later, she'd given it to a friend. She never seemed worried over being bald after that incident.

To me, the woman outside of that shop that day had been an angel delivering a message my daughter had needed to hear. In spite of all that Jessie had been through, she was beautiful to this stranger, who didn't see her as a girl with cancer, but as a woman in control, making choices in her life.

Rain had needed to feel that and it was yet another blessing we encountered along the way.

*　*　*

45

During this time Lauren decided she wanted to return to public school. I was both disappointed and relieved by her decision. When I'd gone back to work during the divorce, my two older girls had opted to continue to home school in the evenings and on weekends, rather than return to the public school system. Lindsey had chosen to be in the regular school system since kindergarten, but even with Lindsey in public school, I was straining to spend the time I needed to on both Newt and her sister's schooling, especially with the additional demands of Jessie's care.

"I don't want a GED, Mom. I want a diploma," Lauren had insisted as we moved deeper into the summer months, continuing our homeschooling even while her friends vacationed, because we were still behind schedule.

"You'll have to test back in," I said. "I'll find out what we need to do."

"Thanks, Mom."

"Of course, honey."

August brought the release of the first book of my trilogy, which meant a workshop and autographing for me, and admissions testing for Newt. She had numerous tests for the different subjects.

I pressed my phone to my ear as I waited in a dark paneled room of some educational building while Newt finished the last of her testing. "So, she passed the science one, as well?" I asked the woman on the other end of the line. She was coordinating the testing.

"She did. She's done very well. This is rare that a student would receive this much credit testing back into the school system from a home school environment. We don't usually see that as the case."

Pride swelled in me. "Well, she's an incredible kid. I can't really take the credit. She's worked hard for this."

And so when Lindsey returned as usual to public school in August, Newt reenrolled and returned with them, and Rain continued home schooling through her chemo. We were in a state of transition as she moved out of Dr. Nelson's care and we looked to the transplant team to guide us through the next phase of her treatment.

CHAPTER FIVE

More Doctors, More Questions

THE OFFICES OF THE BLOOD AND marrow group weren't too different from the oncology clinic, except instead of a waiting room full of patients, only a few earlier arrivals dotted the padded chairs lining the small entry room. A curved counter resided at one end. We checked in as others arriving after us moved to the opposite end of the room to disappear through an inner door.

The receptionist gestured to a bottle of hand sanitizer sitting on the counter beside a box of surgical facemasks. "Please clean your hands before entering the clinic area."

We did as instructed and in time found ourselves in a back office sitting before Dr. Bradford. He was a little younger than Dr. Nelson and seemed capable.

I doodled on my notepad alongside the questions I'd written for this appointment. I'd, of course, researched stem cell transplants and discussed my findings with Jessie. Though I insisted she be in the driver's seat as far as the decision-making process, my role was to advise her as thoroughly as possible. Still, with the abundance of information available, it wasn't easy finding all that was pertinent to her particular scenario.

Dr. Bradford described the procedure she faced, much as Dr. Nelson had relayed. I made sure Dr. Bradford communicated directly with her by not making eye contact with him and keeping my focus on Jessie while he spoke.

Then he added, "You might experience temporary damage to your heart and lungs."

I'd read this and had prepped Jessie for it. "But you'll be monitoring that as she goes. Her lungs have already shown some damage."

"Yes and I discussed that with Dr. Nelson, who says her pulmonary function tests show it's minimal. She's young and that will help with her recovery. She may possibly come through it without any further complications to her lungs, but you should be aware of the risks involved."

"Dr. Bradford, when she first started this, I read Hodgkin's lymphoma patients had a ninety percent survival rate. So, I understand the ABVD wasn't effective, but where does this put her now, as far as that?"

He frowned. "Did Dr. Nelson not discuss this with you?

"I didn't ask him about survival rates since her...relapse." I still had trouble with the word. In my mind a relapse occurred after the disease in question had been overcome. Jessie hadn't come close to that.

"Let me give you some perspective on this." He paused again, as though choosing his words. "Most people diagnosed with Hodgkin's lymphoma are cured using the ABVD regimen, roughly two-thirds of them. Cured, meaning they never relapse."

Again, he paused and I held his gaze. I didn't like the feel of this conversation. If he had bad news, better I bear the brunt of it than Rain.

He continued, "Of the remaining one-third who relapse, most relapse after completing chemotherapy, usually years after. That Jessie relapsed during treatment shows us we're dealing with a particularly aggressive case of Hodgkin's."

He sat back and I glanced at my pages of scribbled notes. I should have researched rates of relapse. I should have better prepared her for this. Still, we needed to know how dire the situation was.

"So, as far as survival rates, what are we talking now?" I'm not sure why I pressed him, but I needed to know what odds we had to beat.

He shook his head. "I don't like to put a number on anyone's survival. Too low, they give up; too high, they don't take treatment seriously. Odds don't mean anything. Individuals beat them all the time."

Rain leaned forward and spoke for the first time since we'd entered. "If you were to put a number on it, though?"

Dr. Bradford turned to her. His gaze fixed on her for a long moment. "If I had to give a number I'd say with this procedure, you have a thirty percent survival rate. Without it..." He spread his hands, palm up.

"Thirty?" I asked, my stomach clenching.

Jessie's gaze remained steady. She nodded. "Without it I die."

"That is the likely outcome."

"So, I do the transplant."

"I don't see where you have much choice." He leaned forward and gestured to my notepad. "I see you've done your research, so I'm sure you're also aware of the fertility issues involved."

I glanced at Jessie as I gathered my composure. *Thirty percent.* I couldn't dwell on that now. I needed to stay focused on the discussion at hand and we hadn't discussed the fertility issues. I'd been more concerned with the life threatening aspects.

But Jessie wanted children, four to be exact. Even at eighteen, she'd been planning them for years, having already chosen their names and sexes, as though she could dictate if she had girls or boys.

When she'd started her chemo with Dr. Nelson I'd looked into cryopreserving her eggs, but in those days the procedure was still experimental. Eggs are fragile and don't freeze well on their own. Success rates for cryopreservation didn't support the cost of the procedure. And at that point we understood she faced the risk of infertility, but she also had a fair chance she'd come through chemo capable of bearing her two girls and two boys, so we'd taken our chances.

Dr. Bradford leaned toward us. "Chances of infertility with the high-dose chemo are around ninety-five percent." He paused a moment to let that sink in. "In light of that, would you like to speak to a fertility specialist?"

Though he'd addressed the question to Jessie, I immediately answered, "Yes."

At the same moment she shook her head. "No."

I turned to her. "But, honey, you want kids."

Again she shook her head. "Look at me. My genes are all screwed up. I shouldn't pass them on to innocent babies."

My heart squeezed. She was thinking not only of the Hodgkin's, but of the great trauma she'd experienced the previous year. "You don't know that. We can talk to the specialist and then you can decide."

She pressed her lips together but made no further protest. Dr. Bradford wrote down a name and number. I took it from him and thanked him.

"You'll need to see him as soon as possible. We only have a little over two weeks before she starts her high-dose chemo. Please let me know what you decide. If she goes through fertility treatment, we'll need to coordinate her care."

"Of course. We'll keep you informed," I said.

* * *

The following morning, Jessie and I again sat in front of a desk in yet another office, waiting for the doctor of the day. She shook her head as I pulled my trusty notebook from my bag. I needed it to take notes. I hadn't had time for research. I'd called Dr. Thomas right after we spoke with Dr. Bradford and here we sat.

"I still don't think I should do this, Mom," Jessie said.

I nodded. "Okay, you don't have to. It's completely your decision, of course, and I'll support you whatever you decide, but please at least think about it. If you don't do anything now, you'll likely come out of the transplant sterile and if that's what you want, then that's fine. Like I said, it's your choice to make. But remember, if you do something now, that doesn't mean you have to have children later. It just means you'll hopefully have a choice."

The doctor entered, preempting her response. He introduced himself as Dr. Thomas, and then took his seat. "So, you're interested in in vitro fertilization?"

I straightened. I hadn't thought of that as an option. I'd still been thinking along the lines of cryopreserving her eggs.

Jessie said, "I'm not sure I want to do anything. I don't know if I want to have kids."

"That's why for the past five years or so you've been planning to have two girls and two boys and have even chosen names for them." I nodded to the doctor. "We spoke briefly yesterday when I called. Please, tell us her options. I hadn't realized she could go through in vitro fertilization. I researched cryopreserving her eggs before she started the chemo."

"The eggs on their own are too fragile. They don't withstand cryopreservation well. Most aren't viable. If we fertilize her eggs, though, she stands a better chance," Dr. Thomas said. "I have to tell you honestly, though, based on our conversation yesterday, it doesn't look good."

"Because I have bad genes," Rain said.

"Because you've never had a regular cycle, you're on the pill and you've had a significant amount of chemo." He ticked the reasons off on his fingers.

We'd had to start her on the pill years ago to help regulate her cycle. We'd kept her on it not only to continue to regulate her, but also because we couldn't risk a pregnancy during chemo.

"I know it doesn't look good," I said. "But is there a chance?"

He spread his hands. "There's always a chance."

I nodded. "Then if Jessie is agreeable, I say we do this."

He looked to Jess. "So, young lady, what do you say?"

Her gaze swept from mine to the doctor's. Slowly, she nodded. "Okay."

*　*　*

"Mom, I need your help." Jessie summoned me to what we called our schoolroom. It had originally been the formal dining room, but since we ate mainly in the kitchen, we'd replaced the hanging light with a regular ceiling light and set up desks and computers along the walls.

She sat at the desktop. "What was that website Dr. Thomas's nurse gave us?"

She grinned and ran her hand across the short strands covering her head. Her new hair was growing in baby-soft. "You know, the one with the donors. I want you to help me to pick one."

Anticipation radiated from her, and I smiled as I navigated to the website and logged in with the secure password they'd given us. I was pleased she wanted to include me in this endeavor. "Sperm shopping on the net. Unbelievable."

She nodded. "You really can buy anything online these days."

I scrolled down the screen, scanning our search options. "What are you looking for?"

"Tall, six feet or over."

"Of course." I clicked the dropdown menu and made the selection. "Hair color?"

"Blond."

"Eyes?"

"Blue," she said in a dreamy tone.

"You do realize you'll never meet this man?"

"Yes, I know."

"And the chances of you having a blond-haired, blue-eyed child are fairly slim."

She nodded. "I know."

"Okay." We finished inputting her search criteria and I hit enter.

"What have we got?" she asked as the results displayed. She straightened. "They don't have pictures?"

I shook my head, smiling. "You don't get to see what the donors look like."

"That sucks. Okay, let's start at the top. Who's first?"

"Ah, we have donor 1729." I moved the mouse. "Let's see his medical history."

"Wait. Look, pictures." She pointed to a link.

I clicked it and a fair-haired youth grinned at us from the screen. "He's cute."

Jessie frowned. "He's, what? Four? No current pictures?"

"Sweetie, you know they're anonymous."

"But what are the chances of me bumping into him and recognizing him?"

I nodded toward the screen. "None, with pictures like that."

"Voice." Again she pointed to a link. "That's so cool. I want to hear him."

I clicked the link.

"Hello, how are you today?" A smooth baritone greeted us.

"Nice." She nodded, smiling, her eyes lighting up.

A laugh bubbled up inside me. "Remember we're not man shopping. Even if he's a blond-haired, blue-eyed Nordic god, we only want his sperm."

She chuckled. "Yes, but I still have my standards."

"Sure you do and I know you want a healthy donor."

"Yes, I do." She gestured toward the mouse. "Okay, let's see his medical history."

We compiled a short list as we clicked through the possible donors. Jessie made notes as we went. I clicked on another voice sample. We listened intently as donor 3690 recited, "Hello, how are you today?"

Jessie crinkled her nose. "Too nasally. My kids are not going to talk through their noses."

"No problem." I clicked out of his profile. "We have other options."

"That first one, number 1729 is my first pick so far."

We vetted the rest from her search results and I passed her the list of hopefuls. "Is number 1729 still your first pick?"

She took the list and consulted her notes. "Here." She ranked her first five picks, and then handed the list back to me.

I clicked on donor 1729's profile and shook my head as I selected him for our shopping cart. Who knew at a time like this we could have fun online shopping for sperm?

A pop-up message opened and Jessie groaned. "He's out of stock?"

I laughed. "It seems your man is in high demand."

"Well, is he, like, back-ordered?"

I scanned the page. "Sorry, hon, he's just out of stock. No projected date for a new shipment, besides, you don't have time for a back order. We have just a two-week window to get this done, remember? Let's try your number two guy."

She sighed. "Okay, but 1729 was hot."

"He was too good to be true. No one has medical history that clean. He's either lying, or he isn't involved enough with his family to know his real background. Neither is a good scenario."

"You're probably right," she said. "I'm better off without him."

"Exactly. Oh, look, your number two, number 1878, is in stock."

"Which one was he?" She looked over her notes. "He's tall, has green eyes...we could have green-eyed children."

Funny, until she was about eight, I'd thought of Jessie as having brown eyes. Then one day we'd been in our backyard, surrounded by green grass and she'd been crying. She'd looked at me, with tears rolling down her cheeks, venting some serious emotional trauma. All I could say was, "Your eyes are so green. Why have I never noticed you have green eyes?"

She'd stopped her tirade. "I do?"

Now, I touched her hand. "Yes, you could have green-eyed children."

She smiled and I tucked the smile away for later. We'd had so few smiles lately.

We'd returned to the fertility clinic for Jessie's first treatment the day after meeting with Dr. Thomas. As she met with the nurse, another nurse showed me to a small office where a young woman explained my payment options.

"Dr. Thomas is discounting his fees because of Jessie's situation, and we're donating all of the drugs she'll need." She waved her hand. "We get samples all the time and won't have any trouble there."

"We appreciate that. We haven't had time to really think about this, much less plan or save for it."

She nodded. "I think it's a wonderful thing you're doing for your daughter."

"How could I not? For years she's been planning on having kids. I want her to have choices later in life, when she's ready."

The woman slid an invoice across her desktop. "Here's your total, with the breakdown in cost."

She moved her pen toward the bottom of the sheet. "Here's the discounted amount."

I reviewed the breakdown and, in spite of the discount, the hefty total at the bottom. My gut tightened. I had no idea how I'd come up with that amount, but at the moment I didn't care. Jessie deserved this.

The woman said, "That's about half the going rate. So, how would you like to pay?"

I pressed my lips together, then straightened, almost laughing as I asked, "Do you take Visa?"

"Mom?" Jessie drew me back to our shopping. "Are we ready to do this?"

I gave her a smile. "Yes. I'm glad you decided to go through with this, hon."

She nodded as she sent number 1878 to the shopping cart. "Like you said, it doesn't mean I have to do anything with it, but maybe I'll have a choice later."

I pulled my credit card from my purse when she reached the pay screen. "One day I'll tell my grandbabies how we bought them with my Visa card."

Jessie arched her brows. "Well, they aren't quite babies at this point."

Warmth filled me. "Not yet, sweetie, but they will be."

* * *

The next week and a half flew by. Between gearing Jessie up for the high-dose chemo and the fertility treatments, I administered her up to five shots a day. I hated that we'd both gotten so comfortable with needles. At one point I had the nurse draw a bull's eye on Jessie's backside, so I'd know exactly where to sink the largest needle of all. We were both wary about this particular shot. It was the big finale.

"Are you ready?" I asked as I angled the needle, aiming for the center of the circle.

She glanced back at me, a look of resolve firmly planted on her face. "Yes. Do it."

I sank the needle in, the way the nurse had instructed.

"That's it?" Jessie asked.

I pressed in the plunger, dispensing the contents, and then withdrew the needle. "Yes."

"That wasn't so bad."

"Really? It didn't hurt?"

"Not so much," she said.

I frowned as I stared at the needle. "I'm sorry. Maybe I did it wrong."

"Are you saying you're sorry you didn't hurt me more?"

I chuckled softly. "No, honey, I just want to make sure I did it right."

Jessie straightened and yanked up her jeans. "You did it right."

"Yes," I said. "I got it right in the middle of the circle. And that's the last one. Now all you've got to do is produce some eggs."

Her lips curved into a grin. "Yeah, I'll get right on that."

* * *

On the second Friday since we'd first met with Dr. Thomas at the fertility clinic, I sat in the waiting room while his nurse, Jan, checked Jessie to see if all those shots had helped her to produce any eggs. When we hadn't had results at the start, they'd gradually raised her dosage until I'd been injecting her with the highest dose of hormones they could give her. We'd remained hopeful.

After some time, Jessie joined me and I asked, "How did it go?"

She shrugged. "We'll have to see. She's looking at it now."

We chatted quietly as we waited. Finally, Jan stepped out to see us. "Come on back."

Once we were in her office, she shook her head. "I'm so sorry, but we still don't have any eggs. Sometimes these things take time and I know you don't have much time. It's a race to get her producing eggs and she hasn't been off the pill that long. It just may not happen."

I glanced at Jessie. She'd stopped taking her pill the day we'd first come to the fertility clinic.

"But there's still some time," I said.

Jan sighed. "I'm afraid we can only give her through the weekend. If she doesn't produce any eggs by then, we'll have to call it quits."

Jessie's gaze met mine and I nodded. "We understand."

CHAPTER SIX

Birthday Chemo

Don't forget I have to take off this afternoon again," I reminded my boss, Tom Simons, the following week. "I'll make up the time. We're seeing both the transplant oncologist and fertility specialist. It's like a puzzle, trying to get it all in before the stem cell transplant."

"That's fine." Tom gestured toward his office. "Could I see you for a minute?"

I nodded and followed him. As he closed his office door I refused to worry about the layoffs, even though scores from our Houston office had already been riffed, as well as numerous people from our Atlanta office, including the four other support positions in treasury and finance. I hadn't had seniority and I'd been surprised to find myself the only remaining administrative support for our department.

I settled in a chair at his small conference table before his big window overlooking the tree-filled park below. This was one of the reasons I loved Atlanta. Even though it was a metropolitan area, it was green with trees. I took in the view and remained calm as he settled into the seat adjacent to me.

Whatever was to be would be. Worrying wouldn't do me any good.

"I want to relieve you of any concerns you may have over the time off you need," he said.

I'd explained to him how I'd have to be Jessie's main caregiver during her stem cell transplant and would be dedicating my time to her twenty-four hours a day, seven days a week for a minimum of one-hundred-fifty days. I'd actually signed a document with the transplant team, committing to that schedule.

"I'm not worried," I said. "I'm prepared to do whatever I need to do in order to be with her."

"That's what I want to talk to you about." He paused.

My stomach tightened. Would I be able to take out a second mortgage to sustain us if I were out of work? How quickly could I contract more books?

"I've had several meetings on this." He named our CEO, CFO and EVP of Human Resources. "We didn't have a policy that addresses your situation."

I nodded, uncertain of exactly what he meant or where he was going with this.

"We've done some research on how other companies handle this and we've gotten the process down, so we can institute a new policy."

I frowned. "What kind of policy?"

"You need time. You've used up your vacation days and need more allocated."

I nodded. With Jessie's current schedule, even with working some from home, I wasn't always able to work my forty hours each week and I'd pretty much depleted my vacation bank. Tom had been very flexible with me. He'd already suggested I continue to work from home as much as I could, but once the transplant started, we'd be at the clinic every day. Working would prove difficult.

"You've got your hands full," he said. "And Jessie needs your undivided attention. As much as I need you, I want you to be able to focus on her. I don't want you to worry about work."

"Newt can help me care for her. It won't be a problem for me to work from home, if it's okay for me to work some in the evenings."

"What I'm saying is that we want you to have all of the time off you need to take care of whatever you need to take care of. Work should be the least of your concerns right now."

I waited for him to continue.

"A lot of people here appreciate the job you do. You know I do, but a lot of other people do, as well. And we're all empathetic to your situation." He shook his head. "I don't think any of us can fully comprehend what you're going through."

My throat tightened and I remained silent.

Tom leaned toward me. "We're instituting a policy where people can donate you their vacation time. It'll be something others in need in the company can use going forward. You already have a number of people who have offered to donate vacation hours to you. You'll have a pool of as much paid time off as you and your daughter need."

He settled back in his chair. "If you can give me a schedule we'll get it rolling. HR has already been informed. We're asking Pat to stay on and cover for you in your absence."

Pain seared my throat. The room blurred. Pat was one of the executive assistants who'd been laid off. This would be good news for her, as well. I nodded, unable to speak.

"Dorene, we all want to help. We're glad to have found a way to do so."

"Thank you." At last my voice worked, though the words came out rough and sounded inadequate to my own ears. Tears rolled down my cheeks. It was more than I could have hoped for and I'd be forever thankful.

They were giving me time with my daughter.

* * *

Jan, the nurse at the fertility clinic, smiled as she greeted us that afternoon before Jessie had to start her latest chemo. Dr. Bradford wanted her to have a round of ICE chemo to mobilize her production of stem cells. She was due to start the following week. We'd been holding our breath since our visit to the fertility clinic the previous Friday and Jan's warning that they might have to pull the plug on Jessie's treatment. We were running out of time.

"I have good news," she said.

"All right." Jess grinned. The high spirits she'd been in after our online shopping had waned after our last visit. "I'll take some good news. Please tell me I haven't been a pin cushion for nothing."

"You haven't been a pin cushion for nothing," Jan said.

A rush of joy filled me. "We have eggs?"

Jan held up her hand, fingers spread. "I didn't think she'd do it, but we have five." She shrugged. "We'd like more, but considering a few days ago we were ready to call this off, I'd say five is a good number."

Jessie bobbed her head. "So, Josh, Logan, Torrent and Drizzella all have a chance of being born."

Jan's eyebrows arched. "Drizzella?"

"Drizzle for short," Rain and I answered in unison.

I laughed and shook my head. "Goodness, I hope they're all boys or you come up with different names for your girls."

"Mom, what are you saying about the names I've chosen for my daughters?"

I grinned. "I'm saying I can't believe I'm supporting this when you plan to name my granddaughters Torrent and Drizzle."

Jessie smiled. "You'll love them all the same."

I touched her arm. "Yes, I will, honey."

"You know, we can't make any guarantees—" Jan began.

I waved my hand. "Yes, we know. They may not fertilize and even if we get embryos, they may not be viable. We get that—no guarantees."

She nodded. "Good, okay, so we do the retrieval on Saturday and we'll know by the end of the day if you have embryos."

"We'll have them," Rain said.

I met her gaze and smiled.

* * *

Jessie sat silently beside me as I exited 400 onto Lenox Road, heading toward Piedmont Road, to the office of Terry Cooper, the attorney who'd handled my divorce. I was updating my will and Jessie was having him draw one up for her.

She turned down the radio. "There's something I want you to promise me."

I glanced at her, curious. "And what is that?"

"If anything happens and I'm not around to use my college money, I want you to use it to pay off the fertility treatments."

My stomach tightened. I hated when she talked like this. "Honey, you're going to be around."

"But in case I'm not. It's important to me that you use that money to pay off your credit card. I don't want you to be in debt because of me. I'm going to tell the attorney I want to leave that money to you in my will and I want you to use it for those expenses. Okay?"

I turned into the office complex's parking lot. "*If* anything should happen to you, which it isn't, then I'll use that money to pay off your fertility treatments."

"Okay, but I want you to promise."

Frustration had me gritting my teeth. "I don't like you talking like this, but, yes, I promise."

"Thanks, Mom."

I merely nodded. It really bothered me when she spoke in this way. I didn't want her projecting anything but the best scenario for herself.

Moments later we entered the attorney's office and, after a short wait, his assistant showed us back to his office.

"Dorene, it's good to see you." Terry Cooper rose as Jessie and I entered. It was late September, two days before Jessie's nineteenth birthday.

I shook his hand then turned to Rain. "This is my daughter, Jessie."

He motioned us to seats in front of his desk. "So, you want to update your will and we're drawing one up for Jessie?"

"That's right." I touched Jessie's arm. She should be out with her friends, not sitting here, but she'd been the one to first mention drawing up a will, even before the transplant clinic recommended it.

"How old are you?" Terry asked Jessie.

"Eighteen, but I'll be nineteen in a couple of days."

He smiled and gestured between us. "You know your mom looks more like your sister. Hopefully you'll age well like her."

"Hopefully," Jessie said, her gaze downcast.

"But it's a good thing you've decided to go ahead and create your will. I know people twice your age who don't have them."

"I just thought it would be a good idea," she said.

"You're pretty young. It's a little surprising you'd be even thinking about a will."

She glanced at me.

I leaned toward the attorney. "She's been diagnosed with Hodgkin's lymphoma. She's undergoing a stem cell transplant. The transplant clinic is recommending it."

I turned to Jess. She gave not a hint of fear or grief over her circumstances. She took on her ordeal without missing a beat.

He nodded slowly and said to Jessie, "I hope everything goes okay for you."

"Thank you."

"So, let's get started, then. I'll need to ask you a few questions." He pulled a pen from his pocket. "I'll draft the documents based on your answers and then, when we have them the way you want, we'll meet again and formerly sign everything with witnesses. Does that sound good?"

"Yes, that'll work." She relaxed a little in her chair.

"And do you know what a living will is?" he asked.

"Yes, and I want one." She glanced again at me.

I nodded my reassurance. Knowing this was a necessary task didn't make it any easier for either of us. "She also needs to do a power of attorney."

The attorney made a note on his pad. "Okay, then let's get started."

* * *

I settled into the molded plastic chair beside Jessie. She got the comfy recliner, along with the other patients at the blood and marrow clinic. They sat in rows, separated by curtains, all plugged up to IVs. She was having mobilization chemo to get her producing more stem cells. She'd had surgery the previous day and today's chemo was administered via her new central line the general surgeon had implanted into her chest.

After her surgery, the nurse had explained to me how to flush out the two external tubes should I ever need to. She'd said, "They should keep them cleaned out at the clinic, so you shouldn't have to worry about it, but you should still know how to do it."

She gave me a bag full of saline filled syringes then handed me a big metal clamp. "Keep this on hand, just in case. If anything should go wrong with either of the valves, you'll need to stop the blood flow immediately."

I'd stared at the instrument, hating the need to have it and praying I'd never have to use it. My poor Jess had never cared for the portacath in her arm and now she had this new hunk of metal in her chest. And I was the proud owner of a surgical clamp, so I could stop her from bleeding to death, should the need arise.

I turned to Jessie. "I'm sorry you have to do this on your birthday."

She shrugged. "It's cool."

"Not really." I shook my head. "It sucks."

"It's okay. You're spoiling me tonight, right? I get to take a break from home schooling today and we're ordering in whatever food I want and you made a cake."

"And you get to pick the movie."

She nodded. "Right. And I get to pick the movie."

"I can't wait." I grinned and she laughed. Jessie picked the worst movies. I straightened. "And we're still celebrating your three cryo-babies."

"Yes, I'm glad you talked me into that, Mom."

I leaned toward her. "Even though I stuck you a million times and you only got three, not four, and they may not even be viable?"

"Yes." Her gaze held mine. "Thank you, Mom. One way or another, I'm going to pay you back one day."

I waved my hand, not wanting to think about her will. "Yes, you'll give me grandbabies, but for now I'm happy with cryopreserved embryos. Happy birthday, Jess."

"Thanks." She gestured toward my book bag. "So, are you going to read to me, or what?"

I pulled her book from my bag and opened it. "Of course."

⁂

I was obsessed with cleaning, consumed by my concern over Jessie being home after the stem cell transplant with her immune system depleted from the high-dose chemo. I wanted the house sterilized from floor to rafters. Tension filled me as I knelt on the linoleum, scrubbing with a sponge dipped in a pine-cleaner solution, because I didn't feel regular mopping would get it clean enough.

Jessie sat at the kitchen table doing her schoolwork. She was having a fairly good day. Her friend Cytney was visiting. I sat back on my heels, dropped the sponge in the bucket and rolled my shoulders to release some of the pressure between my shoulder blades. I hadn't worked this hard when Jessie was a newborn and we brought her home from the hospital.

"That's it," I said. "I'll think of you as a newborn."

Rain stared at me, her eyebrows arched. "What?"

"I'm just thinking about after the high-dose chemo for the stem cell transplant, when I bring you home and you don't have an immune system. I'm feeling like I have to sterilize the entire house and that's stressing me out."

"I'll be fine, Mom. Don't stress."

"I'll clean like I did before I first brought you home. I was pretty thorough then. You survived."

"That's right."

"Yes." I focused again on scrubbing the floor. I'd clean the best I could. I'd be thorough, but I wouldn't stress about it anymore. She was right. She'd be okay.

The water rippled outward from my sponge as I dipped it again in the cleaning bucket. "You know I really believe you'll be fine, Jess, and I want you to really believe it, too."

She glanced at Cytney and then at me. "I know that."

I rose and stripped off my rubber gloves. I sipped from my glass of water I'd left on the kitchen counter. "Seriously, your thoughts and intent have power."

This wasn't the first time she'd heard this from me. She nodded. "I know." She gestured toward my water glass. "That's why we always drink your water. It tastes better, because you bless it."

"Right." Between her talk of her Viking burial and her will I had to make her really believe in her ability to beat this cancer. "Have you guys seen the frozen water crystals?"

Cytney perked up. "You told us about them, but I haven't seen them."

Cytney and Rain had become friends during a summer camp we'd held some years before and Cytney had been a part of our family since then.

"Come see," I said. I glanced at Jessie's schoolwork. "This is educational."

I led them to the desktop computer in the schoolroom. "Let me see if I can find it."

I searched for "frozen water crystals Japanese scientist" and found the website for Dr. Masaru Emoto. "This Japanese doctor experimented with exposing water to different stimuli, like words, music and prayers, and the different exposures changed the structure of the water when he froze it into crystals."

"That's so cool." Cytney leaned toward the screen as we scanned through pictures of unformed crystals affected by heavy metal music and then the pristine images of crystals affected by classical music.

"Look at these," Jessie said as we viewed the disfigured crystals produced when exposed to the word "evil" and then the beautiful crystal ring resulting from the word "angel."

"See," I said. "The body is what, seventy-something percent water? Our words and thoughts have power in the physical world, creative power. That's why you have to believe, like I do. I believe you'll get better, but you need to believe it, too."

Cytney smiled. "I believe. That's awesome."

Jessie nodded, her gaze serious. "Okay, Mom. That's cool. Thanks for showing us."

"Good," I said before I headed back to my cleaning, leaving them to look through the crystal photographs.

The following morning I entered the kitchen to find Jessie, black marker in hand, writing on a cup. Water bottles and other cups were scattered across the countertop.

"What are you doing?" I asked.

She handed me her water bottle. "I'm making sure my water is all good."

I turned the bottle in my hand. The word "vitality" was written in Jessie's scrawl across the front of it. Other water bottles had words like "healing," "strength" and "love" written on them. She'd written similar words on the cups.

"Is it okay if I do this?" Jessie asked, stopping to glance over all the cups on which she'd already written.

I smiled. The cups were plastic and recyclable. Even if they'd been crystal wine glasses I would have been thrilled. If this was what it took to keep her of a positive mind, I was all in. "Of course it's okay."

* * *

About a week later, I kissed Lindsey's cheek as I pulled the blanket over them. Then I sat on the bed beside them. "I'm so sorry I missed seeing you the other morning for character dress-up day. Newt said that you wore the medieval gown she made."

Years ago, when Lauren had decided that she wanted to learn to sew, I'd suggested starting her with a simple A-line skirt. In typical Lauren fashion, though, she'd taken on the medieval gown and it had turned out to be absolutely gorgeous. She'd no doubt pinned it up for her little sibling to wear.

Lindsey nodded. "We had a parade. Everyone liked my costume the best."

Having finished her high-dose chemo, Jessie had had the transplant that day. The event had actually been anticlimactic after all the buildup leading to it. The nurse's biggest concern had been to keep her warm during the procedure. The stem cells had been thawing but were still very cold as they reentered her system. We'd kept her wrapped in blankets during the process as the nurse slowly administered the stem cells through her central line with an instrument that, to me, resembled a turkey baster.

I was mostly apprehensive about the aftermath of the high-dose chemo. The drugs' affects had been brutal on Jessie so far and we were all watching her closely. Her condition was deteriorating by the hour.

"I hate that I couldn't be there," I said to Lindsey.

"It's okay. Jessie needed you. I understand."

"I still would have liked to have seen you."

"I like it when Newt helps me." They turned to their side and nestled into the pillow.

I smoothed their hair. "Me, too, honey."

A wave of regret swept over me. I was missing so many of the special moments of their lives, and Lauren had practically abandoned her childhood to help care for her siblings. Would I ever be able to make it up to them?

After saying goodnight to Lindsey, I headed downstairs to mix up Jessie's nightly cocktail of pills, consulting my list to make sure I had the correct dosage for her blood thinner. Rain sat on a stool at the kitchen counter and stared at the medicine cup full of pills, green ones, pink ones, yellow and white.

I handed her a cup of water, one on which she'd written "Happiness." "You can take them one at a time. You don't have to do them all at once."

She nodded as she turned the cup slowly and the pills rattled against the side. She'd prided herself on being able to down all of her meds at once, like throwing back a shot. The oral bulsafan and high-dose IVs were taking their toll on her gastrointestinal tract, though. She had trouble swallowing water, let alone pills, and she couldn't shake the cold that had seeped all the way into her bones.

She took a sip from the glass. Her eyes teared and she grimaced as she swallowed. She drew a deep breath. "I can do it."

"Sweetie, just try to take one pill. If you can't, it's okay."

"The doctor said if I can't swallow I have to go to the hospital," she said, her frustration evident. "I hate the hospital."

"I know, hon." She was no doubt remembering her stay towards the end of July. She hated being sick, but even more, she hated depending on other people to care for her.

"Remember, Matilda at the clinic said it wasn't a matter of if, but when you'd go to the hospital. It happens to all of the transplant patients."

She pressed her hand to her forehead. "But I don't have a fever."

I sighed. I didn't want her in the hospital any more than she wanted to be there, but this high-dose chemo was debilitating her. She seemed in pain with every movement.

"You haven't eaten today."

"I had a little pudding—"

"A bite doesn't count."

"I drank a little of that protein shake."

"That was this morning and again, a few sips don't count," I said. I nodded toward the medicine cup. "If you can take them, you can stay home tonight. If you can't, I'll call the nurse and she'll most likely tell us to take you to the hospital."

Her eyebrows furrowed. She took another sip and held the water in her mouth as she tilted her head back and dropped in the smallest of the pills, a quarter of a tablet of the blood thinner.

I held my breath as she struggled for a moment, then spit the pill fragment into her hand. Tears welled in her eyes. "I can't."

I rubbed her back, hating the chemo. My poor girl could barely swallow her own spit. "It's okay, sweetie. I'll call the nurse."

CHAPTER SEVEN

In Search of a Donor

A FEW DAYS LATER I ENTERED Northside's oncology unit, grabbing a blue paper gown and matching shoe coverings from a stack inside the heavy doors separating the unit from the rest of the hospital. I moved to the sink in the adjacent restroom and washed my hands the way the nurse had instructed the night Jessie had been admitted, counting to twenty while I rubbed soap over all sides of my hands, rinsing them thoroughly, and then using a paper towel to turn off the faucet before drying my hands under the blower. To this day I catch myself counting while I wash—twelve, thirteen, fourteen—a constant reminder of those days at the hospital.

Not until I was properly garbed and cleaned did I use my elbow to push the button for admittance through the final set of doors into the sterile unit. Jessie's room was off the main hall on the right. I passed a couple of other patients with family members helping them to walk laps around the ward. Maybe Jess would be able to increase her laps today.

"Good morning," I greeted her as I entered.

She grimaced. Dark rings circled her eyes. I pulled a chair to the side of her bed. "Did you sleep at all?"

"No." She shook her head. "I hurt all over."

They'd started her on a new pain medication the previous day, since morphine had made her itch uncontrollably. "I'll talk to the nurse about your pain meds and maybe they can give you something to help you sleep. Has the doctor been by yet?" I always tried to walk Lindsey to school then make it to the hospital before morning rounds.

Jessie frowned. "You don't need to talk to anyone. I already spoke with the nurse."

"But, honey, we should let them know you're still in pain. Are you using the button the way the nurse showed you?" I gestured toward the remote beside her with the button that released her pain medication as she needed it.

"Yes, I'm pushing the button. I don't need the nurse."

I hesitated, torn between wanting to get the nurse and honoring Jessie's wishes. She was in obvious pain, but I'd always told her she was in the driver's seat and if she didn't want the nurse, I wouldn't get the nurse. Jessie seemed especially testy. Better to tread lightly.

I shifted my book bag from my shoulder to the floor. "You can take a break from school today and I can read to you, if you'd like."

Her chest rose and fell. She closed her eyes. "Read to me, please."

I found where we'd left off the day before. I'd been reading for maybe twenty minutes when she groaned, still in obvious pain. I put down the book.

"Honey, if it hurts, you should push the button to self-medicate."

"I know how it works," she snapped.

"Then did you push the button?"

Her gaze swept to the clock on the wall. "It isn't time yet."

I leaned forward and kept my voice soft. "No, hon, there's no timing. The nurse said to push it when you have pain. You're having pain. You should push it. There aren't time intervals. She was very clear on that, remember?"

She glared at me. "I know what she said, but I'm doing this my way."

Frustration flooded me. I hated seeing her in pain and it was unnecessary. Somehow I had to help her see past her own stubbornness. She didn't need to suffer. "But your way doesn't seem to be working. Maybe you should try it the way the nurse said."

"I want you to leave. I don't need you. I don't *want* you here."

The vehemence in her voice momentarily stunned me. I couldn't leave her. "Sweetie, I'm just trying to help you."

"I don't need your help." She nearly rose with agitation as she pointed to the door. "Leave! I don't want you here. Get out!"

Her words and aggressive tone brought tears to my eyes. My gaze swept to the door. The doctor and one of the nurses stood in the open entryway, shock raising their brows as they stared at us. My cheeks warmed with embarrassment.

The doctor was the first to recover as he stepped into the room. "Now, here, what is this?"

"She has to go," Rain said, anger roughening her tone.

To my further frustration, I couldn't stem the flow of tears running down my cheeks. I sat rejected and mortified. I inhaled in an effort to compose myself.

I rose. "It's okay; I'll give her some space."

"No." The doctor held up his hand to stay me as he turned to Jessie. "I understand you're going through an awful time here, but that's exactly why you need the support of your family. I'm going to have to insist that your mother stays. Doctor's orders."

Jessie clenched her jaw and didn't respond.

"It's okay," I said again to the doctor, before moving beside Rain. I touched her shoulder. "I'm going to grab some breakfast downstairs, and I'll come check on you later."

She responded with the slightest nod of her head. I inhaled as I left, breathing through the heaviness that had settled in my heart. All Jessie wanted was a little control over her life. I got that, but it still hurt.

* * *

Somehow we survived the week of that hospital stay, where once again, she'd forbidden me to call any of her friends. We segued into our new normal, which was life posttransplant. This consisted of daily trips to the clinic and my constant worry over Jessie's lack of an immune system.

"I've got that," I'd said the first time we reached a doorknob after she started high-dose chemo. Then I'd jumped in front of her in the elevator of the parking garage to press the button for our floor. At home, I walked around disinfecting countertops and ensuring every item out of the dishwasher was bone dry before being put away. Anyone with a suspected sniffle was banned from the house. I even required the healthy ones who visited to wear surgical masks just to be extra sure.

We placed her in a bubble. Her safety sphere included home, the clinic and the route in between, where she wore a surgical mask and I didn't allow her to touch anything. We went deep into isolation.

Then the unthinkable happened. While Jessie continued to suffer the brutalities of the high-dose chemo, the lump returned. Dr. Bradford ordered another CT scan two days before Thanksgiving of 2005.

His expression was grave as he reviewed the results with us. "The masses have returned to her neck and chest. There's one area I'm really concerned about that appears to be possibly infiltrating her lung."

I'd given up having him speak directly to Rain at that point. No matter how we diced this it was bad news. "So now what?"

His gaze moved to Jessie, who sat silent and still beside me. "I'm recommending a second transplant, an allogeneic transplant using donor cells this time."

We'd heard this sometimes occurred with transplant patients, but I couldn't imagine her having to go through this again and so soon after the first one. I caught Jessie's eye and could tell she had the same thought. She was exhausted and frail. How could she possibly endure another round of the high-dose chemo?

"Ideally, the donor stem cells would come from someone in her family," Dr. Bradford continued. "Our hope would be to find a match with one of her siblings, but I'd like to have you all typed."

I turned to Jessie. "It's up to Jess on what we do, but I think typing is a good idea."

Dr. Bradford shifted. "And her father. Parents are a fifty percent match. Of course, we'd like to have a higher match with a sibling or other donor, but worst case scenario we could use a parent. Will her father get typed?"

Jessie met my gaze. Larry hadn't participated in the blood drive for the massive amount of platelets she'd needed during the first transplant. If he hadn't been able to donate platelets, how likely was it he'd be able to donate her stem cells?

"I don't know," I said. "We'll have to ask him."

"I think you and her siblings should go ahead and get started with the typing. Meanwhile, I'm referring you to Dr. Adrouni at Northside for radiation therapy. We're hoping the radiation will buy Jessie some time until we find a donor or determine a new course of action."

"Jess?" I held her gaze. "What would you like to do? Should we move forward with the blood typing?"

She nodded and the exhaustion in her eyes spoke volumes.

I turned back to the doctor. "I'll bring Lauren and Lindsey in tomorrow if that works."

"Yes," he said. "That would be good. The sooner the better."

* * *

Thanksgiving was a quiet affair, with just the kids and me, with Phoenix as our one outside guest. Family and friends had wanted time with Jessie, but more people meant the higher risk of her catching something from someone, so we'd deliberately kept it small. Jessie had insisted that Phoenix come, though. She'd be stronger at Christmas and we'd open up the celebrating then.

I was horrified to learn that before coming to our Thanksgiving celebration Phoenix had doused himself in bleach to make sure he was sterilized. He'd also shaved his head in a show of solidarity, since Jessie was completely bald at that time, though she hid it that day under a beanie. When he arrived and saw she also had no eyebrows or eyelashes he disappeared into the bathroom with a pair of tweezers and returned shortly after with bare eyelids and no eye brows, as well.

We spent the day together, talking, laughing, cooking and eating. As I cleaned up the kitchen and the kids sat around the table at the end of our feast, Newt brought out the video recorder. Everyone was in high spirits at that point, talking about the kinds of things kids might talk about at such a gathering.

"Green ones and red ones and..." Jessie grinned and turned to Phoenix.

"Bright orange, though," he said.

"Oh, yeah."

Lauren giggled. "Have one for rainbow."

Jessie gestured with her hand. "No, but the solid green. Those feel good to get—"

"You said green?" Lindsey asked, disbelief in her tone.

"Still eating," Newt said.

"Green," Jessie repeated. "Orange is normal. Red's a little strange."

"Wait, purple's normal, but red's a little strange?" Lauren asked.

Laughing, Jess said, "No, I said no purple. Red's a little strange."

"Purple's kind of close to green." Newt panned the camera between Rain and Phoenix as Lindsey laughed.

Phoenix couldn't resist his curiosity any longer. He lifted the gray beanie from Jessie's head. She sat quietly while he revealed her bald head.

"Yeah, I know, there's not even a shadow or anything," she said, grabbing the beanie and tugging it back into place, her gaze slipping to the side.

Looking back on that video it strikes me first how happy they seemed on that day, in spite of everything. I also can't help but notice how much off center Jessie's jaw was, though I hadn't noticed it at the time. Certainly, it was more crooked than when I'd dragged her to all the orthodontic surgeons and even the chiropractors.

How much of a factor could the chemo have played in the further torquing of her spine, evidenced by her increasingly crooked jaw and her loss of over an inch in height? Did this shed light on the excruciating back pain she'd suffered during her first hospital stay in July of 2005?

* * *

We'd all gotten typed for the second transplant and we'd been wrong about Larry. He agreed to being a possible donor after discussing it with Jessie. This was fortunate, because I had a condition that made me a high-risk donor and we'd been surprised to learn that both Lauren and Lindsey had been less than fifty percent matches.

"Is that unusual?" I'd asked Dr. Bradford.

"It happens," he said. "I'd hoped that wouldn't be the case, but, no, it isn't unusual to not find a match among siblings. I've already started a search in the national donor bank, though, so we'll just have to wait and see."

"Her blood work looks good." One of the clinic nurses smiled during a daily visit not long after that. "She can get outside and take a short walk, as long as she avoids contact with other people."

"A walk?" Jessie repeated, frowning. "That's it?"

The nurse nodded. "Yes, a walk for now, which can be really nice."

I leaned forward. "I'll go with you. Some fresh air would do us both good."

Rain nodded, obviously disappointed. I, on the other hand, was happy with the prospect. I loved walking with my kids. When they'd been little, we'd taken many walks through the neighborhood and local parks. I always walked on the outside, so I was on the side with the traffic, explaining it was to keep them safe.

Once, when Jessie had been about thirteen, the two of us had been walking and she'd slowly moved to the outside, leaving me on the safer side. Her feet had outgrown mine when she'd been nine and she'd topped my height when she'd been ten. By thirteen, she towered over my five feet and two inches. I'd glanced at her askance when she'd maneuvered to the traffic side.

81

"The cars won't even see you," she'd said.

Of course, I still kept an eye out for cars. I possibly should have been insulted, but instead, my motherly pride had me beaming. It had been a turning point in our relationship. I'd loved how she was growing into adulthood in that moment.

Yes, a walk with my Jess would be a welcome activity for me.

"You'll be able to go out in public soon," the nurse said. "It won't be too much longer before it'll be okay to plan something limited, depending on her blood work, of course."

Jessie straightened in her recliner, where she was plugged up to her special IV of the day. "Can I go to the movies?"

My stomach tightened as I imagined the crowds of people at the movie theater. We'd kept guests limited at the house and when they had come, I'd asked them all to wear surgical masks. Having her around the general public seemed more than my nerves could take. I shook my head and exchanged a look with the nurse.

But the nurse's smile didn't falter. "I had a patient once who had a private showing at a theater." She turned toward me. "Do you have a regular movie theater where you like to go?"

"We have a couple of places in our area."

"You could call the manager at one of them and ask for a private showing just for Jessie," the nurse said. "We could probably allow that in the not too distant future," she said. "Again, depending on her blood work, of course."

"Yes, Mom, please. *Goblet of Fire* is coming out and I really want to see it."

I hesitated for only a moment. The clinic wouldn't okay it if it were too risky for her. "Sure, honey, I'll ask."

* * *

"You'll wear a mask," I said on December first, then nodded at Jessie's hands. "And gloves, the entire time."

Her eyes widened. "Yes, yes. I know. I will."

I heaved a sigh and steeled myself. "Okay. Ready?"

A smile curved her lips. "Yes. I can't believe they're doing this. Thank you so much for asking them and for taking me, Mom."

Her joy was enough to have me swallowing my doubts and heading out the door. We drove the short distance to the AMC Theatre near our home. Jessie had been chafing against her limited boundaries. My own sphere had been limited, as well, with only brief outings to the grocery store while Newt watched over her sister. The rest of the time I'd remained in isolation with Rain.

I was looking forward to our outing, but my protective mom instincts had kicked into high gear. I paused as I parked the car. It may be a private showing, and we'd leave out of the exterior exit, but I still had to get her through the lobby. Though we'd scheduled the movie fairly early in the day, the building wasn't deserted by any means.

"Stay behind me," I said, as we pushed through the main door.

I asked for the manager, who led us to the theater where they were showing "The Goblet of Fire," a special showing, just for the two of us.

He refused to let me pay.

I shook his hand. "I can't thank you enough. This means so much to us."

He glanced at Jessie with her mask and gloves, a cap pulled over her head, covering the little bit of hair that had started to grow back in. "You're welcome. We're happy to do it."

My throat tightened and I nodded, unable to speak past the lump that had formed there. I'm not sure I ever enjoyed a movie more than during that special showing with my Jess.

Throughout this experience, I'd seen people rise to the occasion, strengthening my belief in the inherent goodness of mankind. This was certainly one of those instances.

CHAPTER EIGHT

A Place of Her Own

THE SCENT OF ROASTED CHICKEN filled the air as I tore romaine into a bowl one dreary December day not too long after that. I breathed deeply, trying to revive myself. After getting Lindsey to bed, then finishing school with Jessie the evening before, I had spent a restless night tossing and turning.

Before I drew a second breath, raised voices burst from the living room. My stomach clenched. Jessie and Lindsey were at it again.

I closed my eyes for the briefest second. The constant fighting between them was hard on all of us, but mostly on Lindsey. Even with their two week visit to my sister's in Orlando at the start of summer break, tension between them and Jessie was at an all-time high.

I hurried toward the ruckus. Lindsey stood in front of their sister, hands fisted. Newt had paused at the foot of the stairs, one hand on the banister.

Jessie eyed Lindsey with nothing short of loathing. "You'd better get the hell away from me. I hate you. If I had on steel-toed boots, I'd kick your head in and stomp on your brains."

The pure hatred in her eyes and animosity of her tone sent a shiver of dread up my spine. The hurt in Lindsey's eyes broke my heart.

We'd tried everything to establish peace between them. I'd run mediations with them and we'd gone to family counseling. As I faced Jessie, the counselor's words drifted back to me.

If Jessie continues to abuse her sister, you'll need to look into other living arrangements.

At the time I'd been horrified. Given her current circumstances that wasn't an option. But something inside me snapped at Jessie's harsh words. Was I to sacrifice one child for the sake of the other? What emotional damage was her abuse causing her sibling?

I turned to Jessie. "Maybe we should consider the counselor's advice. Maybe we should look at alternative living arrangements for you, at least temporarily."

Regret flooded me the instant the words had left my mouth. Rain's anger evaporated. She stared at me, her eyes round with disbelief. "I'm dying and you're kicking me out?"

I inhaled slowly. "First of all, you're not dying and, no, I don't want you living anywhere else. But, honey, you can't treat your sibling like this."

"But I can't stay here," Jessie said. "I need to get away. You hover over me all the time. What about Momo's? Can I go there?"

My heart clenched. How could I send her to my sister's at a time like this? "But you have radiation."

"Can't I get it in Orlando?"

Suddenly the idea of Jessie being away from us, dealing with her illness without me by her side loomed beside the issue of her abusing her sibling. Was there a lesser of two evils here?

"We can work this out. We'll go back to counseling," I said. "You shouldn't go through this without us. We'll find a way to all live together peacefully."

"I can't do it, Mom." Tears welled in her eyes. "I can't stay here with you watching over my every move, afraid to let me out of the house, trying to keep me in a bubble. You can't protect me."

The defeat in her eyes made me want to scream. Yes, I wanted to protect her from every imaginable germ that might take her down in her weakened state. I also wanted to protect Lindsey from being hurt by their oldest sister.

Jessie shook her head. "I can't stay with..." She gestured toward Lindsey. "I'll kill them if I stay."

"Sweetie, I don't want you to go. I'm sorry I said anything. We're all feeling stressed. It's like we're in a pressure cooker here. It's understandable under the circumstances, but we can find a way. We just have to work together."

She shook her head again. "I'm calling Momo."

I held my breath as she left to get her cell phone. Heaviness weighed my heart. Why had I said anything? I couldn't send her away. Not now.

"I'm okay, Mom." Lindsey slipped under my arm and hugged me.

I smoothed my hand over their hair. "She can't treat you that way, hon."

"But it's okay," they said.

I pulled back to meet their gaze. "No, honey, it isn't. It doesn't matter what your sister is going through. It isn't okay for her to treat you like that."

Lindsey's gaze hardened. They shrugged. "I don't care."

"Well, I do. Whatever happens, we have to find a way to work this out. You're family."

Jessie returned, her mouth set in a firm line. "She said no."

Relief shimmered through me. "Honey, you understand it's too much for her to take on."

She drew a deep breath. "What about Larry?"

The knot in my stomach tightened. How was I supposed to let her go? At least her father was local. "Sweetie, if you feel you want to ask him, that's fine, but I don't want you to go."

Her gaze slipped to her sibling. "I'll call him."

She moved into the school room again. Her murmured tones floated to us as Newt took Lindsey by the arm. "Come on, Munchkin," she said as she led them up the stairs.

Jessie returned a moment later, tears brimming in her eyes. "He said no."

I closed my eyes, hurt for her and relief warring in me. "We'll go back to counseling. We'll work it out, so we can stay together peacefully."

"My friends, most have graduated and are either working and living in their own apartments, or are in college. I haven't even finished high school. And I'm still here." Tears brightened her eyes to green. "I haven't accomplished anything."

My heart swelled. "By whose standards are you judging yourself? I believe most souls choose one lesson to learn in each life, but you have already experienced lifetimes of learning in the few short years you've been here. Sweetie, from a soul's perspective, you've done so much."

"Do you really think so?"

"Yes."

She was quiet a moment, her eyes still filled with tears. "I need to know what it's like to be on my own, though. I may never know what that's like."

My throat tightened. All she wanted was to be normal again, leading the life of a regular nineteen-year-old. "You'll know, honey. You have plenty of time for that."

She shook her head. "You don't know that."

I grabbed both of her arms. She couldn't lose hope. "I believe it." My heart thudded dully. "You need to believe it, too."

She shook her head. "I want to know what it's like to live on my own. Just for a little while, Mom. Please. This could be my only chance."

Fear gripped me. No, she couldn't think that way. She couldn't talk that way. How could I let her go, especially now?

I stared at her for a long moment. This was so unfair. We should be arguing about normal things like curfews and boyfriends. The thought of sending her out into the world on her own, without me there to watch over her with her depleted immune system sent dread spinning through me.

Yet, Lindsey and Lauren deserved a break from their sister's abusive flare ups. In addition, during her winter break, Lauren had volunteered to fill in for me with my twenty-four–seven care of her sister, and I'd been spending short periods of time working at the office. During this time Jessie had already snuck out on numerous occasions to public places she shouldn't have gone, even once to the movie theater where she ran into the generous manager who'd arranged her special showing.

We couldn't sit on her twenty-four hours a day. When I tried, it set us both on edge. And Jessie's emotional well-being was always a consideration.

Which was more important at this point?

Finally, I let go of her and stepped back. "Let me call the extended-stay hotel up the street. I'll see if they have any vacancies and how much it will cost. Maybe a little break would be good for all of us."

She straightened, her eyes a glittery green. "I love you, Mom."

"But you have to promise me you'll be careful and won't go out in public."

"I promise," she said, though her gaze slipped to the side.

I inhaled slowly. Having her home hadn't proven fail safe on that front. "And we'll see if Cytney will stay with you."

I at least wanted someone else on hand to help watch over her, and I'd feel better if Cytney were that person.

"Yes, Mom, I'll ask them."

She hugged me tight, again saying, "I love you."

"I love you, too, honey."

* * *

I couldn't afford to pay for that extended stay any more than I could afford the cryo-babies, but prior to that I'd been fairly reasonable with my credit cards. This was important to Jessie and we all needed a break from the constant fighting.

In the end, I gave her one month in the extended-stay suite. Cytney agreed to move in with her, and I saw Rain every day. That went a small ways towards relieving my worry, especially when Cytney got sick and had to cut short their stay with Rain.

Cold air wrapped around me early one morning as I stopped by to get Jessie from the hotel to take her to her radiation therapy. She'd started radiation about a week after Thanksgiving. I pulled my coat close as I knocked at her hotel door. Scuffling sounded from the other side, along with a muffled exclamation or two. At last the door opened and Jessie squinted into the overcast December morning.

"Hey," she said as she slipped on her heavy coat. She tugged her cap over her head, even though her hair had started to regrow. She was always cold these days.

"Morning." I peered past her, to the liquor bottles littering the counter of the kitchenette.

"Ready?" I asked.

She nodded, and then followed me to the car. Fifteen minutes later we entered the radiologist's office and another waiting room. After signing in, we took our seats. It was early and only one other woman sat in a nearby chair.

Jessie yawned and I resisted the urge to ask her about her night. I knew she'd been having people over until all hours, partying like there was no tomorrow.

"Jessie?" a young male attendant called her from a side door. He led us back to an examination room, since we were seeing the doctor today. "Dr. Adrouni will be with you shortly."

We sat in silence for a while, our chairs side-by-side.

Jessie leaned forward, propping her elbows on her knees. "Thanks."

"For?"

"Letting me have my own place for a while and not asking a lot of questions."

I nodded. "Please just promise me you're being careful about having people over and you're not going out in public, or you're at least wearing a mask."

She sighed, her frustration evident. "It means a lot to me you're letting me do this."

"You're going to have plenty of time to experience life on your own when you eventually move out. For now, I'm happy to do this, since it's important to you."

"I know you want to believe that I'll have that opportunity, Mom." Her voice faltered and tears gathered in her eyes. "But I know this is going to kill me."

Her admission hit me in the pit of my stomach. My throat tightened and the room blurred. "No, honey, please don't talk like that. We still have all the alternative treatments to explore. You still have lots of options."

"It won't matter."

"Jess, you have to keep positive."

Tears rolled down her cheeks. "I've accepted it. I'm not going to make it."

I shook my head, unable to speak through the burning in my throat. She couldn't give up. I blinked through my own tears.

A knock sounded on the door and we had no opportunity to compose ourselves before Dr. Adrouni entered. She took one look at both of us and her gaze filled with sympathy.

"Ladies, I'm so sorry to see you're having a bad day, but we're going to do everything we can to help you."

She updated us on the continued course of treatment they had planned. As she spoke, I drew a deep breath. Jessie could give up, but I'd be damned if I'd join her. I'd find an alternative treatment that would work. I'd believe in her recovery twice as hard if needed. If sheer will counted for anything, I'd will her back to good health.

* * *

Though some of her strength was returning, the radiation was hard on Jessie.

"I need more aloe," she said, frowning. "I'm burnt, Mom. My skin is black."

She suffered through as well as she could. That her days of radiation therapy were limited wasn't exactly comforting. This had been a stop gap measure. We still didn't have a clear path to her recovery.

My oldest sister, Marion, had written summaries on several books she'd read on alternative treatments for cancer. Jessie and I had been discussing the different therapies her notes described. Maybe it was time to schedule something along those lines.

"We haven't found a donor yet," Dr. Bradford told us one afternoon at the blood and marrow clinic.

"What are her chances if we do find a donor?" Again, I couldn't stop myself from asking.

This time he didn't hesitate in answering. "The allogeneic transplant has a twenty-five percent chance of helping her beat this."

The knot in my stomach tightened. Her odds were heading in the wrong direction. I should just quit asking.

He inhaled slowly before continuing. "And you should know it has a thirty percent chance of killing her."

I stared at him in disbelief. "And still you recommend it?"

"I do," he said. "It's her only chance."

"No." Jessie shook her head. "I don't want that." She held my gaze. "I'm done. I don't want to do this anymore."

I nodded slowly, my throat tight, the sick feeling spreading through my gut. "Okay."

"I think you should reconsider."

I turned to Dr. Bradford. "We still have the alternative therapies to explore."

His gaze was doubtful, but he slowly nodded.

*　*　*

"I'm thinking I can rent a house with Jack when my month is up," Jessie said one day when we returned to her extended stay after her radiation treatment.

Apprehension filled me. Jack was an old friend she'd run into there. They'd parted on bad terms years ago after he'd gotten into drugs and consequently into trouble with the police. It had really hurt her to lose his friendship.

"I don't know about that, Jess."

"He's changed. I told you, we're okay now."

I'd had to call the police one night after finding a bag of stolen mail in my living room. The police had traced the bag to her friend, Jack, who'd evidently let himself into our house after we'd all gone to bed one night to sort through his bag of stolen mail. I hadn't seen him since those days.

"You may trust him, honey, but I don't," I said. "I don't want him hurting you again. Besides, that's not the only issue here. How are you going to support yourself? And you're still dealing with so much."

"It'll be Jack, me and his girlfriend. We'll split rent. I'll get a job."

"How? How will you get a job? You're still having radiation. And we're not sure what's next, but you have other priorities right now. You have your health to consider."

I hated bursting her bubble, but the reality was that she wasn't able to be independent at this point. Besides, the thought of her permanently moving out sent panic exploding through me, with or without her friend Jack.

She shook her head. "I'll manage."

"Look, honey, I get that you want to be independent, but the timing just isn't good right now. We'll find another way."

She couldn't be serious about moving out. She was still so weak from the stem cell transplant. It could take a full year or more before she was fully recovered.

"I can pull some of the equity out of the house. Maybe we can renovate the basement for you, make it like an in-law suite. Then you can have your own space."

Her gaze brightened. "Could I have my own entrance? Is that even possible?"

Jessie currently lived in the finished portion of the basement, but we all crossed through her space on our way to the laundry room, so her privacy was limited. An in-law suite would give her privacy and a feeling of independence.

"I don't know. I'll talk to a couple of contractors and get some estimates."

"You'd do that for me?"

"Of course, I would. I think you're going to need more time than you realize before you're back to your old self. If we can swing that, you'll have all the time you need to get better.

And I won't have to worry about you trying to make it on your own out there."

She shook her head, frowning. "No, I don't want you going into more debt for me."

"And I don't want you living away on your own just yet."

She stared ahead, her jaw set in that stubborn way I'd learned to dread. I inhaled slowly. "I'll get some estimates and then we'll talk some more."

As the days in her month at the extended stay dwindled, I held my tongue and waited for her to come to the obvious conclusion that she couldn't afford to live on her own yet. Our agreement had always been that her time to move out would be when we were both comfortable with her level of stability. As much as I wanted her to have the independence she craved, right now I wasn't close to comfortable.

Meanwhile, I met with a couple of contractors to see what it would cost to convert my basement into an in-law suite for her. I'd need to also look into an equity loan. It might be a good compromise for both of us.

The first week of February, Jessie checked out of the extended-stay hotel and returned home, much to my relief. I'd received estimates on the renovations, but hadn't yet gotten the equity loan, so she moved back into her old basement bedroom. She passed one hundred days of recovery posttransplant and was slowly regaining her strength. It was time to open our minds to other healing opportunities.

"A road trip to Indiana?" Newt asked as she, Lindsey and I sat at dinner one cold night in mid-February, while Jessie rested in her room. "To that healer, the one Larry sent us the e-mail on?"

"Yes, the Amish horse farmer," I said. "His name is Solomon Wickey."

"What kind of healer?" Lindsey asked.

"He diagnoses people by reading their eyes. He can detect illness in their irises. It's called iridology," I said. "He also uses kinesiology and does this thing he calls a release. And he knows all about herbs."

"But, he doesn't charge, right?" Newt asked.

"Right. He takes appointments a couple of days a week and then accepts walk-ins on Mondays and Wednesdays. People line up early in the morning for miles outside of his farm. He's helped countless people, with everything from cancer to mental illness. He even once cured a king, who traveled all the way from Africa to see him."

Lindsey scooted forward in their seat. They glanced at Jessie's empty chair. "Is he going to heal Jessie?"

I squeezed their hand. "Well, we're going to see. She has an appointment for next Tuesday."

CHAPTER NINE

Road Trip to a Healer

THOUGH JESSIE CAME DOWN WITH a cold the weekend before our road trip to see the healer, I tried not to hover. I watched her as closely as possible, taking her temperature at regular intervals and encouraging her to rest and hydrate. I called the nurse the minute the thermometer indicated a fever. I took her to her doctor, who diagnosed her with walking pneumonia. I held my panic at bay, as we started her on an antibiotic.

I settled in with her, pumping fluids, continuing to check her temp regularly, while keeping her on dose with all of her meds. I checked with the advice nurse about our upcoming trip and in spite of the walking pneumonia, her doctor gave us the go ahead, with our promise to check in on our return and call them immediately if her condition worsened. And so we headed to Indiana, to the Amish horse farmer with the gift of healing.

"You've already been eating the way I'm sure he'll advise." I glanced at Jessie as we sped along the interstate on day one of our three-day road trip.

I'd, of course, researched Solomon Wickey and his advice on treating cancer. We had begun following a vegan, salt-free, sugar-free diet. I'd gone on it with Rain, to support her.

She hated it. Every meal was an agony for her.

"I wonder for how long? When do I get to eat like normal again?"

I shrugged. "You'll probably get to ease up a little in time, but you may need to make some permanent changes."

She frowned as she stared out of the front window. "That sucks. I want real food."

"Well, you want to beat this thing, right?"

She nodded and we drove along in silence. Neither of us had ever been to this part of the country. We were headed almost to the Michigan border, deep into horse country.

We stopped for the night a few hours short of our destination. I felt Rain's forehead as we got ready for bed. "I want to get your temp before you take your meds tonight."

She suffered my hand on her brow but didn't say anything as I pulled out the thermometer. "I can't tell and we need to be sure."

Her temperature was within normal range, though a little higher than I'd prefer. "How are you feeling?"

She shrugged. "I'm fine."

This should have eased my concern, but until we had her through this whole ordeal, I wasn't about to relax.

"Thanks for doing this, Mom."

The gratitude in her gaze warmed my heart. I smiled. "For what? Bringing you on a road trip to see an Amish horse farming healer?"

"Yes."

"Of course, Jess, there's nothing I wouldn't do for you."

"I know."

* * *

I'm not sure what I'd expected, but Solomon Wickey was a small man, direct and to the point. We shared the waiting room with only one other party, a husband and wife, who were return visitors who sang Solomon's praises. They were good people. I sat beside Jessie, grateful we'd been able to schedule an appointment and hadn't had to line up and wait with the hordes.

When our time came to see the healer, he took us into his office, where he sat by a large desk. He asked her to have a seat in the chair beside him. As with our other appointments, I let Jessie take the lead and speak with him about what had brought us to him.

He listened contentedly and then tilted her head as he looked into her eyes with what appeared to be a magnifying glass. He turned to me, his own eyes rounded with disapproval, appearing even larger behind his glasses. "You've shot her full of chemotherapy."

Stunned, I had no reply for him. It was true Jessie had moved forward with the chemo because I'd encouraged her to. I'd been afraid and since we were enrolled in a HMO at the time, this was the normal process with this type of diagnosis.

The fact that we were sitting with an Amish horse farming healer was a testament to our open-mindedness, but I had let my fear cloud my judgment. We'd tried traditional methods first, since they negated many of the nontraditional treatments, but what would have happened had we originally turned to the alternative therapies instead?

"She doesn't have cancer," Solomon said with conviction after he finished his examination. "Anyone who treated her with chemotherapy should be shot."

I glanced at Rain, then back at him. "But they did two different open biopsies and the cells presented as Hodgkin's lymphoma. They said it was in a definite pattern."

He waved his hand. "They don't know what they're looking at."

We can rule out Hodgkin's.

What if the pathologists at Emory had been right?

"Then what is it?" I asked.

"She has too much calcium," he finally said, sitting back in his seat.

"Is that why I'm always hacking up all these hard white things from the back of my throat?" Jessie asked.

"Could be." He nodded.

I blinked. Calcium? Could it be possible we'd been on the wrong track all along?

"Would this cause her lymph nodes to swell?"

His eyebrows arched. "It could. Her body makes too much calcium and it has to go somewhere."

"And is it possible it would cause her spine to torque?"

He thought for a moment before nodding. "That's the rheumatoid arthritis. It could do that. She could have calcium deposits along her spine. Her body doesn't know how to process it."

"Rheumatoid arthritis?" I asked, trying to take in this new information. "Does that have something to do with the calcium?"

"So that's why my jaw is crooked," Jessie said. "They want to cut it out and move it."

"Nonsense." Solomon again waived his hand in dismissal. "All she needs is to take calcium for about four months."

"Wait," I said, fully aware I wasn't allowing Jessie to take the lead. I was completely thrown by all he was telling us. "If she has too much calcium, why does she need to take more?"

"So her body will stop manufacturing it. I know it doesn't sound right, but to lower her calcium levels she has to take calcium."

He shrugged. "I have some here, or you can get it where you want. I'll write down what she needs." He turned again to Jessie. "Is anything else ailing you?"

"I have trouble learning. I think I'm ADHD."

He held her wrist for a minute. "No, you don't have ADHD. You had dyslexia."

Again, surprise filled me. I'd asked her teachers about this in elementary school and had been assured she wasn't dyslexic. She'd had a vision disorder we'd had corrected when she was maybe twelve. She'd become an avid reader after that and I hadn't been too concerned, but Jessie had always wanted a magic pill to help her to focus.

"She's dyslexic?" I asked.

Solomon smiled. "She was, but not anymore."

"I have heartburn and I get congested a lot." Jessie glanced at me.

He held different bottles of what I supposed were herbs up to her or had her hold them while she held her arm in front of her at an angle and he told her to hold firm while he pushed down on it. "Let's add some yucca to her treatment."

We talked to him about that which I'm not allowed to write and he assured us she was okay along that front. Jessie was beyond pleased with his comments.

She glanced at me. "What other issues do I have?"

It seemed she'd been plagued by so much for so long, but now my mind was a blank. I shook my head. In spite of my open-mindedness, I was having trouble trusting what he was telling us.

"I can't think of anything." I turned to Solomon Wickey. "We'll get the calcium and yucca from you."

"We're not done." Solomon motioned for Jessie to get up and then gestured towards me. "You need to come sit here."

"Me?"

He nodded. "I fixed this in her, but it needs to be fixed in you and in your mother and any sisters and any other daughters you may have. It's an abnormality in the eighteenth chromosome. It's passed down on the maternal side. You're a carrier."

He rattled off a string of diseases associated with an abnormality in this chromosome, including Hodgkin's, though he reiterated Jessie was indeed cancer free and that rheumatoid arthritis was the real culprit.

I took the seat and he circled his fingers around my wrist. "I can try to bring in my other children, and I'll tell my mother and sisters, but I'm not sure they'll come."

"You can just send me pictures and I can fix the others. They don't have to come here."

"What happens if they don't get it fixed?" Rain asked, standing behind me.

"It's a calcium imbalance. It can show up as rheumatoid arthritis." He glanced at me. "You don't want that and there's no need. I assure you one of your mother's ancestors had rheumatoid arthritis and if we could trace further back than that, we'd find a point where one of her ancestors had leprosy and that's what damaged that eighteenth chromosome, which eventually manifested as rheumatoid arthritis."

He let go of my wrist. "Now you're fixed, too."

"Thank you," I said. Could I put my faith in this man? At least he seemed confident he had a solution to Jessie's illness, as simple as it sounded. What did we have to lose by trying the calcium and yucca?

Jessie gripped the back of my chair. "So I don't have cancer and I don't have to eat that nasty cancer diet, the one with no meat, no dairy and no sugar or salt?"

"That's a good diet," Solomon said. "And it helps people with cancer. It's what I recommend for them, but no, that doesn't apply to you."

"So I can eat whatever I want?"

"Well, you don't need the cancer diet." He wrote the information for the calcium and yucca on a small sheet, then handed me another with his address on it. "Don't forget to send me those pictures."

"I won't."

I hesitated. I wanted to offer him payment but had read he wouldn't accept it. The last thing I wanted to do was insult the man. "Thank you. I'll pray for you and your family."

He nodded. "Then it's a done deal."

Sometime later we sped along the interstate, on our way to Georgia via Kentucky. Jessie's good mood had dissipated and she leaned against the window on the passenger side. Concern filled me.

I pressed my hand to her forehead. "Oh my God. You're warm."

"I'm okay."

"No, you're not. I can see that. The walking pneumonia..." I wanted to smack myself. "You have walking pneumonia. How did we miss telling him that?" I glanced in the rearview mirror. "We should go back."

"No, it's too late."

"He may still be there."

"Let's just go home."

"Jess, I don't know. Maybe he can make you better."

"I'll be fine. Everything happens for a reason. I didn't think of it either. We weren't supposed to tell him about it."

"But how could we both forget? I was just so thrown off course by that whole rheumatoid arthritis and eighteenth chromosome talk." I gripped the wheel, torn.

If we could have called the man I would have done so, but the appointments were arranged by a non-Amish friend of his, who actually used modern technology. I'd contacted him via email and had to wait for a response. Communicating with the Amish horse farmer wasn't a fast process.

"Just keep driving, Mom."

I drove, but each mile increased my worry as Jessie's condition worsened. I'd called her nurse shortly after we'd decided to stay our course. She'd had me make an appointment with Jessie's doctor for the following day when we'd arrive home. After a restless night and a day on the road with Jessie's continued deterioration and another call to the nurse, though, I ended up driving her straight to the emergency room upon our arrival to Atlanta the following night.

We had a long wait after being on the road all day, but we finally saw a doctor. Poor Rain was miserable by then.

"We'll start her on a new antibiotic," he said. "I want to give her a little via IV, but I'll also write her a new prescription." He nodded toward Jessie. "You can sleep in your own bed tonight. No need to admit you."

"I feel like shit," she said.

"We'll do the IV. I'll send in a nurse to get you started."

Jessie turned to me after he'd left. "I can't believe they aren't admitting me."

"That's a good thing, honey."

But a couple of hours later, after the IV, she was still miserable and nearly in tears. "That didn't do anything. They can't fix this."

I rubbed her back. "Let's get you home. I'll Reiki you."

She nodded and my heart clenched. If I could take this on in her stead, I'd do it happily. It just wasn't fair that she had to go through so much.

* * *

Nearly a week passed after that trip to the ER. I could barely get Jessie out of bed. She continued to run a fever.

"I'm so cold," she said, her arms wrapped around herself, blankets nearly burying her. "I hurt all over."

"I know this isn't any fun. I'm going to call the nurse again and let her know the new antibiotic is still not working." I'd called several times throughout the week and they'd advised us to give the antibiotic more time to work, but Rain couldn't wait any longer.

"I don't care what the nurse says. They can't help me."

I sank to the bed beside her. "Honey, I know you're miserable, but they *can* help you. The doctor can help. Maybe they can take another X-ray of your lungs."

"What good will that do? I don't want to go to the doctor. I don't want to move." Tears streamed down her cheeks.

My heart swelled for her. "I'm so sorry, honey, but you aren't going to get any better staying in bed."

"I'm not going anywhere. Nothing they try helps. I hurt all over. I'm not leaving here."

Frustration welled up in me. This wasn't the first time we'd butted heads over her care.

"Please, Mom, don't call the doctor's office."

I stared at her a long moment. I'd told her at the start of this that she was in the driver's seat. I just didn't agree with where she was driving herself at the moment.

Her voice hardened. "I won't go if they want me to come in, so don't waste your time. Just leave me alone."

"Fine." With my frustration morphing into anger, I left. I had two other children who needed my attention. It felt too much like banging my head against a wall with Jessie today.

But my concern didn't abate and as the afternoon waned I resolved to try once again with her. When I found her still huddled in bed, I was at least heartened that she had enough energy to be angry.

"I told you to leave me alone."

"I'm not leaving you alone. It's too late to go to the doctor and I've had enough of this. I'm taking you to the hospital."

Her eyes narrowed. "I'm not going to the hospital. You can't make me."

"Yes, I can." My five feet and two inches might not stack up against her five feet and eight inches, but she was weak and

I had a mother's resolve. "You're not getting better and the nurse said to take you in."

"I told you not to call the nurse."

I squared my shoulders and faced her. "I don't care what you told me. I love you and I want you to get better, so you're going to the hospital. Now, am I dressing you, or do you want to dress yourself?"

Jessie didn't pull out any stops that night. She bitched the entire time until we left the house and the entire drive to Northside Hospital. At one point, I was so fed up with her verbal abuse and constant insistence that I turn the car around, that I actually considered taking her home. Then my worry over her condition had me gripping the wheel and focusing on the road ahead.

"They won't be able to do anything. They didn't help last time. They're a bunch of idiots."

"They're trained medical professionals and now they know the antibiotics didn't help, so they'll try something else."

This time they took her pretty quickly in the ER and then it wasn't long before she was admitted to the oncology ward. I paced in her room, unable to settle into the chair beside her. "You should let me call Tabby and Anna this time. Not right now, it's too late for tonight, but tomorrow."

"No. I told you before...I don't want you...calling anyone." She closed her eyes as though pained.

"Jess?"

One of the nurses rushed into the room and to her side. "I'm really concerned about her stats. I'm coding this and we're going to have the team evaluate her. They'll probably move her to ICU."

"I don't understand," I said.

The nurse fixed her gaze on me. "She has fluid in her lungs and filling the area around her lungs and heart. She's going into respiratory arrest."

An alarm sounded. My heart thudded as the nurse moved again to Jessie's side. In less than a minute the room filled with people in scrubs. They surrounded my girl. I couldn't even get close to her.

Our dear family friend Barbara Karraker, an IV nurse thankfully on duty at the time, stepped beside me. "Her lungs aren't functioning adequately. They'll probably have to intubate her."

"What does that mean?"

"They'll put her on a ventilator to help her breathe until her lungs clear and she can breathe on her own."

I wrung my hands as the first nurse moved beside us, her gaze serious as she said, "ICU is full, so they're taking her to CCU. They're getting a room ready for her now."

I glanced at Babs as they settled Rain into a wheelchair. Babs squeezed my arm. "She's going to be okay. You got her here in time."

Horror filled me. I'd come so close to turning the car around. It seemed to take forever, but when her room was ready I grabbed our things and rushed to Jessie's side, hurrying along with her entourage as they wheeled her to the cardiac care unit.

She looked at me and I could nearly feel her fear. Her words came out haltingly as she struggled to breathe. "They want...to shove a tube down...my throat."

"They want to help you breathe, honey."

"And if I don't...let them am I...going to die?"

The nurse beside her glanced at me before answering, "If you don't go on the ventilator, your lungs will cease to function."

"And I'll die." Her voice was barely a whisper.

I pressed my lips together as Jessie finally nodded. "Okay."

By the time we got her to the CCU, and our friend, Babs, had helped her prepare herself, Rain was nearly in a panic. She was struggling for each breath. Tears rolled down her cheeks. "Are they...doing the tube thing? I can't...breathe."

I nodded. "They're getting everything ready. They're going to have to sedate you, but I'll be here with you. I'm not going anywhere."

"Can they do it...now?"

I'd never seen her so afraid. Not through chemo when she first got sick and lost her hair, not through the transplant when she was here in the oncology unit in dire pain, coughing up tissue from her esophagus and unable to swallow her own spit, and not through the radiation that blackened and blistered her skin and had her spitting up blood.

As I moved to the side, her team took over. In spite of my promise to Jessie to stay put, one of the nurses escorted me down the hall and into a waiting area. Apparently, they didn't want me around while they intubated her. In the flurry of activity, I hadn't gotten to say anything more to Jessie.

It was after one in the morning by then and I was exhausted. I'd called Lauren earlier to let her know we'd be at least staying the night. It was too late to call anyone else. I'd update them in the morning. Jessie didn't want me calling her friends, but I'd at least call Larry and the rest of my family. While I waited, there wasn't much else for me to do.

So I prayed.

Eventually, the nurse returned. "You can come back now."

I followed her to Jessie's room in the CCU. I inhaled slowly as the nurse left and I stood alone in the room with my Jessie. She lay unconscious, plugged up to the monitors, the tube down her airway helping her breathe, the incessant mechanical inhale and exhale of the ventilator filling the room.

CHAPTER TEN

Day Bleeds into Night

"DORENE, I JUST WANTED TO LET you know we're organizing a schedule for everyone to take food to your kids," Wendy Wax, an author friend of mine, said over the phone the following day.

I was a member of Romance Writers of America and I knew Wendy through our local chapter, Georgia Romance Writers. At that time, Wendy headed our published authors' group, the Georgia Romance Authors Network. I'd been keeping the group informed of Jessie's progress, since I'd called on them for help during Jessie's blood drive. They'd turned out in numbers, along with work friends, who went in response to a flyer another friend at my office posted on our behalf. I'd be forever grateful for all the support.

"Thank you, Wendy. I feel like I'm abandoning Lauren and Lindsey, but I just can't bring myself to leave Jessie right now and there's no telling how long she'll be here."

"I wish there was more we could do. We have people lined up to take them food every day. They'll just ring the bell and leave whatever they bring on the porch, so as not to disturb them. If there's anything in particular they want or don't want, just let me know. If every day gets to be too much, we can cut it back."

"I'm sure they'll be happy to have whatever people bring. Larry will likely bring them with him to the hospital, but it's hard for me to be away from home. It makes it so much easier knowing you guys are looking out for my children. I can't thank you enough," I said.

"We're happy to do something to help. Just keep us informed on how you're doing. We're all thinking about you."

"Thanks, Wendy, I will."

I hung up and headed back into the CCU. Larry was supposed to stop by and I wanted to give him the latest update.

I slowed as I approached the nurse's station. He stood inside with one of the nurses and he had Lindsey with him. Tension filled me. I'd asked him to give me a chance to talk to Lindsey before he brought them. I wanted to prepare them, so they wouldn't be shocked to see her sister plugged up to all the machines.

He stepped into the hall as I drew near, his eyes red-rimmed.

"I thought you were going to wait to bring them," I said, glancing at Lindsey as they watched Jessie through the glass window that took up the wall of the nurse's station facing Rain's room.

"They wanted to see her. The doctor said..." his voice faltered. "He said that Jessie might not make it."

Anger surged through me, sparked by my continuing state of denial. The last thing Jessie needed right now was for anyone to generate negative energy around her health. "And you told that to Lindsey?"

"They should have a chance to see their sister."

"I wanted to prepare them, so they wouldn't be scared when they saw her."

I drew a calming breath. Getting angry with him wouldn't help anything. I needed to get everyone onboard with keeping a positive attitude. A defeatist attitude wouldn't do Jessie any good. I believed it could actually do her harm.

"We still have the alternative therapies. She is not out of options," I said.

"Mom." Lindsey entered the hall and wrapped their arms around me.

"Hi, sweetie," I said as I hugged them back. "Where's Newt?"

"She's in with Jessie." Lindsey pointed past the nurse's station window into Jessie's room. "Can I go in and see her, too?"

I glanced at Larry and then turned back to Lindsey and nodded. "Okay, though I guess you saw she looks a little scary with all those tubes and everything. She's breathing through that big one and getting medicine through some of the others, and the wires measure how she's doing. The doctors are working to get her better, and we're going to try some of the alternative therapies as soon as she's up to it."

Lindsey nodded. "Can we go in now? I know she can't talk to me with that tube down her throat, but I just want to say hi."

"Then let's go tell her hi," I said as I led them into Rain's room.

* * *

<u>Saturday 3/4/06</u>
Jessie had Lasix® today to help relieve her of the twenty plus pounds of fluid she's been retaining over the past week, since they rushed her here to the CCU. I haven't left the hospital

since, and I don't plan to leave until she's safely moved from this unit.

The Lasix worked almost too well. The fluid came off quicker than her heart could comfortably manage and her heart rate peaked a few moments ago somewhere in the mid 150s, not quite as high as Sunday night/Monday morning, but high enough to give me a good scare when the alarm again sounded and the nurses and doctors hurried to her room. This coding wasn't something I'd ever get used to or wanted to experience again. She's at 142 now and it's slowly dropping. Other vitals look good.

God, I really don't like having her here. The one blessing is that she's so sedated she'll hopefully not remember any of this.

Her nurse has just inserted a feeding tube for the fourth or fifth time. I've lost track. The goal is to thread it in through her nose, down her throat, past her stomach and then into her small intestine, but the line has been curling in her stomach. We'll know if this attempt is successful once radiology takes another picture then reports back. Here's hoping they got it right this time.

She's been coughing a lot, so maybe all of the shaking up she had today has cleared her lungs some more. Though she's breathing on her own for the most part, she's being helped by the ventilator. It blows in pressure to open her airways, and then forces oxygen deep into her lungs with each breath she takes. The machine now provides her with half the oxygen she's breathing as opposed to the hundred percent she started with six days ago.

So, she's made some progress, but the tests she had yesterday and the day before to see if she was ready to begin weaning didn't yield promising results. Hopefully, now that she's shed some of the residual fluid in her system we'll see better results tomorrow.

* * *

Sunday 3/5/06
Looks like Jessie will finally get fed through her newest tube this morning. The last X-ray shows that the tube is right at the juncture of her small intestine, so they're going to give it a try.

Her temp is at 101 something, so Ramona has drawn more blood and collected a sputum sample to culture. My sister Maureen and friend Patti have suggested that Jessie could be detoxing from her trip to see Solomon Wickey, something I've also considered. I still want to kick myself for not asking him to heal Jessie's walking pneumonia while I had the chance. Who knows? Maybe if I had she wouldn't be here now.

It breaks my heart to see her lying in this bed, tubes running from all parts of her body. Several times today she stiffened and opened her mouth, the tears rolling from the corners of her eyes tearing my heart. I will never forget her silent crying, her agony. It's so unfair. She's suffered so much already. Why this?

Even though I've promised myself to stay out of the nurses' way, it was very hard for me when she cried again a short time ago while they repositioned her. The nurses seemed oblivious to her tormented expression. I asked if we could lower her sedation enough to ask her where she was feeling the pain.

The other night they'd lowered her sedation to the point that she'd been lucid enough to tell me through my questioning and her nodding and moving her hands that she was having pain in her stomach. Her nurse had given her more pain medication and Jessie had slept the rest of the day.

* * *

"Ms. Graham?" Ramona, Jessie's nurse for the day, entered the room, frowning. "You have a visitor."

113

"I do?" I glanced toward the door.

"Yes, a young man. He's in the unit waiting room."

"Oh. Thank you," I said. Whomever it was had evidently skipped the outer Family Center and had likely entered the unit without first speaking with staff. No wonder she was frowning. "I'll go out to him."

I glanced at Jessie and though she was unconscious, said, "I'll be right back, honey."

A moment later, I turned into the small waiting area. I'd met other visitors in the bigger room outside the CCU: my boss, Tom, and another writing friend and her daughter who'd stopped by to check on us, but only family had been back this far.

"Hey." Todd, a friend of Jessie's, turned toward me as I entered, concern written all over his face. A doctor and an orderly stood to the side, arms crossed.

I nodded to them. "Thanks."

Todd waited until the two withdrew before saying, "I just heard that Jessie was here, and I jumped in my car and came straight here. How is she?"

"She's been better. They had to put her on a ventilator. She isn't conscious."

He frowned. "What happened?"

"Her immune system was depleted after the stem cell transplant. She got pneumonia and couldn't kick it."

"But she'll be okay?"

I hesitated. The staff certainly hadn't sugar-coated anything for me. Still, I refused to give up. "I believe she'll be okay."

I did believe it. I had to. I refused to give credence to any other belief and I didn't want anyone else doing so. Maybe if enough of us believed hard enough, the creative power of our collective consciousness could help her pull through this.

"Can I see her?"

Jessie *liked* this guy. When she woke up, she'd be thrilled to hear he'd stopped by, but she'd likely want to kill me for letting him back to see her in her current state.

"I'm so sorry, Todd. She wouldn't let me call anyone when she was conscious. She's all hooked up to tubes and things. She's not looking so good. She wouldn't want you to see her like this."

He straightened, evidently disappointed. "I'm leaving for military police training. I won't be back for several months."

My heart went out to him, but I still didn't think Jess would want him to see her. "I'm sorry, Todd."

His expression fell. "Okay, I understand. But you'll tell her I stopped by?"

"Absolutely, as soon as she wakes up I'll tell her. They're working on a plan to get her off the ventilator now. I'll definitely let her know you were here, and I'm sure she'll be happy to hear it."

I hated sending him away like that, but I felt strongly that I needed to respect Jessie's wishes and I truly believed she'd want it this way. I couldn't wait to see her smile when I told her about her visitor, though.

The news would make her happy.

＊ ＊ ＊

Monday 3/6/06
Acute respiratory distress syndrome is what the doctors tell me Jessie is suffering from. She may or may not have pneumonia in conjunction with this, though they are treating her for that, as well.

She was fever free last night and though her chest X-rays don't show much difference from yesterday, her stats show gradual improvement. Her oxygen from the ventilator is now set at forty percent, the lowest it's been and within range to start weaning her.

Tomorrow we'll see how she tests functioning on her own without as much help from the ventilator. If she does well, we may get her off the ventilator altogether.

Nona, another of the nurses, has backed off Jessie's Ativan®, so we can wake her. She's been heavily sedated since yesterday afternoon. Yesterday morning she was semi-lucid, but kept biting her tube, so they'd sedated her a little more. Today, we want to wake her more to get her ready for tomorrow's testing. She'll need to be more conscious to breathe on her own.

The tube from her chest has completed draining but the one on her left side is still draining. In fact, they've just changed out the collection container because the original one was full.

Nona is cleaning her mouth, and she's starting to respond to verbal requests. She has a tendency to bite down and not let up until we've asked her several times to do so. I'm sure it's a natural response to bite the tube when she wakes enough to find it's there.

Jessie was crying again earlier and though it still breaks my heart, I think I took it a little better this time. I talked to her, though she wasn't awake enough to respond or possibly even hear me, telling her not to be afraid, explaining that the drugs made her feel weak and unable to move and that she still couldn't speak, but that she's okay and getting better. I told her what day it was and how long she's been here and updated her on the plan to wean her from the ventilator. I told her I was still here and not going to leave her.

* * *

Tuesday 3/7/06

It's around 8:40 p.m. and once again, Jessie is zonked. She had the tube pulled around 2:40 p.m. She never quite woke up, but she was trying her best, while two of the respiratory team hovered in the area, waiting. Finally, she raised her head and part of a shoulder, and they deemed her ready for extubation.

What a relief! She's been stirring long enough to mumble and moan and warm up her vocal chords, but hasn't gotten her eyes more than half open. Now, she's sleeping. Earlier, she managed to mumble that she needed to pee. I smiled and reminded her she had the catheter. Then I asked her if she remembered coming to the hospital, and she shook her head. With luck she won't remember any of the past week or so.

* * *

<u>*Wednesday 3/8/06*</u>

Jessie is much more lucid today and her speech is getting better, though I often have to ask her to slow down and try to move her lips. Susie, one of the nurses, says Jessie has to relearn how to use her tongue and lips to talk. Her muscle movement is returning slowly. Seems she can move her arms somewhat and her head, but she is slow and not as accurate as she will be.

I can tell she's frustrated that she's still helpless in a lot of ways. It may take days before her fine motor skills return. For now, she's letting the nurses and me help her to do every little thing. It is as if her spirit was so far from her body while she was sedated it is resettling again almost like a newborn's.

Last night I was concerned that she seemed to be seeing things and said she vaguely remembered me. I attributed most of it to the drugs and Susie confirmed that. This morning Jessie seems more oriented and has told me numerous times she loves me and even asked for a hug at one point, which I was thrilled to give her. I, of course, can't seem to stop telling her I love her at the slightest opportunity. I am seeing more of her old self in her this morning, though she is still very disoriented.

She asked what country we were in after seeing Keun, a male nurse, and we both smiled when she said it looked like we

117

were in China. She'd told me last night that I was speaking Japanese and asked who was standing beside me when no one was there. I told her she was seeing an angel, because I'd called them all in to help protect her and that my sister Carol had sent her own guardian angel to watch over her.

It's 4:00 p.m. and Larry left with Lauren and Lindsey a short while ago. He brought books from his sister, Carol. Jessie cried twice while they were here, and I explained to them and again to her that part of this is probably a release of all the trauma of the past couple of weeks and lingering effects of the drugs.

She has coughed up some blood and though she's coughed some more and the blood has cleared, a radiation tech has just left after taking another X-ray.

She's anxious to get back to her old self, and I've told her she has to be patient. She's still very weak. Tomorrow she may be able to sit up, and she may be able to try to drink some water. Keun has told her she needs to be more awake and stronger. Even though she had earlier asked me to unstrap her, free her of all the wires and tubes so she could go to the bathroom, she agreed tiredly to rest, and then shortly after fell asleep.

* * *

Larry kissed the top of Jessie's head. "It's good to see you awake."

"Thanks, Dad."

"Maybe now we can take that trip to Costa Rica," Larry said.

Dismay filled me. Why would he want to take her out of the country in her fragile state? "She can't travel."

"But I promised."

"That would be so cool, though." Jessie smiled.

My stomach tightened, but I refrained from further argument. Surely it was obvious to them both that she was in no condition to travel.

Lindsey stood beside me at the foot of the bed, while Lauren sat on the bed on Jessie's other side, carefully avoiding the various tubes and wires. "Maybe you'll get to come home soon."

Jessie shrugged. "Hope so."

She glanced at me and then leaned toward Larry, her tone too soft for me to make out what she was saying. He, in turn, glanced at me and nodded. "Yeah."

I cocked my head, but Larry's attention was back on Jessie. Ramona, Jessie's nurse for the day, entered. She shook her head and motioned Lauren off the bed. "That side rail should be up." As she moved to Jessie's side, Larry shifted to the foot of the bed, beside me.

"What was that?" I asked.

"She asked if you were really her mom. She said you look too young."

"She doesn't remember me?" I asked, stunned. She'd been a little disoriented at first, but I thought that had cleared as she'd become more conscious and functioning. I'd been fawning over her, hugging her for the past two days since she'd awoken, and she didn't remember me?

But she'd hugged me and told me she loved me. Was she just feeling she needed to reciprocate the outpouring of affection I couldn't help showering on her? And how could she think I looked too young when I'd aged a thousand years since we'd entered the hospital?

But the part that knotted my stomach was that evidently she remembered her father. Me, the one who'd stuck to her like glue through all of this, she didn't remember. I hated to be disappointed, but the hurt was all too real.

"It's probably still the drugs," he said.

I nodded. Of course it was, but I was way too emotional these days to be rational. I'd have to be respectful of her lack of memory until she remembered me.

CHAPTER ELEVEN

Missing Home

*T*HURSDAY 3/9/06

Jessie didn't sleep much last night. Her pain level was at about 5.5, so I asked Susie to give her something for the pain. I had hoped this meant Jess would rest easier, but every time I awoke, which was every couple of hours or so, she was wide awake. Finally, shortly after 4:00 a.m., I sat down to read to her, knowing Babs was going to try to stop by when she got off from her other job, around 4:40 a.m. She came and we had a nice early morning visit.

Jessie's still pretty weak, but her motor skills are improving. Yesterday, she could hardly touch her chin with her hand, but today she can flex her fingers and even scratched her nose. We're celebrating every little victory.

She drank a banana strawberry smoothie earlier and food services just left her lunch tray. Hopefully, they brought some macaroni and cheese, as her face lit with expectation when the doctor said she could eat soft foods and the nurse assured us she'd requested Jessie's favorite.

Two women from physical therapy came by to asses her and run through some exercises with her. It seems her biggest issues are that her feet are "dropping" and that she is still very weak. Tomorrow Jessie will have special boots to train her feet to flex again and splints for her hands to help her straighten her fingers.

Per Dr. Rinner, our focus now is 1) nutrition—she needs protein to rebuild her muscles, 2) physical therapy and 3) rebuilding her strength. She really doesn't need to be in CCU anymore, but the nurses are fudging to keep her here. I think they've all got a soft spot for my Jessie. They don't often see teenage girls in the unit and the staff has gone out of their way to see she has the best care.

＊ ＊ ＊

I inhaled deeply as I stood over Jessie as she lay sleeping. I glanced at the monitor. Her stats looked good. I should eat.

Moments later I padded into the hospital's large open cafeteria. Sunlight streaming through a window caught my attention. *Outside.*

I stepped onto a small exterior balcony, blinking into the soft morning light as it spilled over the area. A slight breeze blew and birds sang. It was a gorgeous day. I let my gaze scan the blue sky with its puffy white clouds. Compared to the cold wet night when I'd brought Jessie here, this day was balmy.

It was spring. I calculated the days since our arrival, stunned as the realization hit me. Two weeks. I'd been inside this hospital for two weeks solid without stepping outdoors. I'd been so focused on Jessie that I hadn't even thought about it until this moment.

Amazingly, in spite of the battle we waged in the CCU, the world had continued its orbit. Winter had melted away and brought this beautiful spring day. I soaked in the warmth and the sunshine, fortifying myself for the days to come.

* * *

Monday 3/13/06

Jessie is still not ready to be left alone, so it looks like I'll be spending another night here with her. Saturday afternoon she was moved from the CCU into a room on 3 North, where we'd started that first night when I'd rushed her to the emergency room. We've been riding an emotional roller coaster for most of the time since she's "awoken" from the ventilator.

Her biggest issue, I believe, is that she hasn't been able to sleep for more than a few hours here and there. She's been distraught at times, rude at others and sometimes really pissed off. I can't blame her, though. I've been sleep deprived myself, though I escaped Saturday afternoon with Lindsey to take them to Moe's then to see "Failure to Launch" and actually spent the night at home after spending more time with Jessie.

Lauren stayed with Jessie that night and though I managed one good night of sleep, Jessie was miserable and upset on my return. I've had my hands full keeping her calm and making her comfortable.

* * *

Tuesday 3/14/06

I miss home. I miss Lauren and Lindsey. I feel torn every night when I think about spending another night away from my other children. Lindsey is holding up okay, though some nights they call to tell me they miss me and can't sleep. I stay on the phone with them for as long as it takes to help us both feel okay about spending another night apart.

Of course, I wouldn't dream of leaving Jessie sooner than she's ready. She says she feels safer with me here and though she makes great progress every day, she still needs help with some of the most everyday things. No, I couldn't leave her here alone.

She walked with a walker out into the hall and back today. I was apprehensive, since this morning when she walked to the restroom in her room and back her heart rate climbed to 160 again. The two nurses working with her raced into the room, but her heart had started to calm by then. Anyway, she managed okay on her hall walk, with the two physical therapists beside her.

Every day we find a new victory. Like when the occupational therapists visited to see how her exercises were going. Instead of her required exercises, Rain had taken to tweezing her eyebrows. When she demonstrated for them, they smiled at her progress rather than chastise her for not doing the exercises they'd prescribed for her.

A wound-care specialist visited her today, and they dressed the wound beneath her left breast where the tube had been. They used a special drain. It's supposed to last for three days, but she's leaked again through her gown already.

Jessie continues to be frustrated but isn't as agitated today as she's been. It helps that she started a new medication to help her to sleep and she slept a little better last night, though she was a bit loopy, and that she napped most of the morning.

Using the bathroom is almost tortuous for her, though, and she's resisted eating and drinking. I finally got her to agree to eat a Hovan, and Larry brought it when he and Lindsey visited earlier. It was great to see Jessie's face light up as she took her first bite.

* * *

The TV played softly as I closed my journal and moved to Jessie's side as she lay quietly watching something on Animal Planet. I felt her forehead.

"I don't have a fever," she said matter-of-factly.

"I'm just checking."

"Right, because they don't check that every few hours around here."

"They're taking good care of you." I reached for her book, one of Sherrilyn Kenyon's latest. I knew Sherrilyn through my writing group, and she was one of Jessie's favorite authors. I'd been happy to arrange a meeting at a signing earlier in the year, and Jessie had been completely star struck.

"Do you want me to read to you?"

She nodded. "But there's something I have to tell you first. It's really important."

"Okay." I frowned, but lowered the side rail and settled on the bed beside her.

She held my gaze. "The staff is really good here. Everyone's been great—here and everywhere else—all of the nurses, the doctors, the alternative healers, everyone has been wonderful, but the only reason I'm still here is because of you."

My throat tightened and I smiled as the room blurred. Jessie could be hard to get along with, but when she loved you, she let you know it. It filled my heart to have her appreciate my efforts after all we'd been through.

I gripped her hand. "Well, I'm not going anywhere. I'm going to keep holding on as tight as I can for as long as you need me to."

"Thanks, Mom, I love you."

"I love you, too, honey."

* * *

Saturday 3/18/06
Jessie's taking her first shower in the three weeks since she's been in the hospital. It should make her feel loads better, and she's already feeling better today. I had hoped to get her discharged yesterday, though.

Unfortunately, she's been running a fever again, 101.7 this morning. And her latest X-ray showed increased infiltrates in her left lung. She had CT scans yesterday, and it appears more fluid has collected around her heart. The thoracic surgeon had been ready to sign off on her, but he told Jessie last night they'd have to keep her at least through the weekend.

Another pulmonologist has been called back in and Dr. Michaels, Jessie's regular pulmonologist, visited this morning. I was surprised when he said the nurse called him at 3:00 a.m., because the radiologist felt she needed to be moved back into CCU. Dr. Michaels had spoken to the pulmonologist who'd seen Jessie after 6:00 p.m. last night. That doctor had said she looked fine and she does. Everyone who's seen her has remarked on how good she looks.

Though she's not back to her old self by any means, she's much stronger today, getting up and moving with plenty of energy. I'm hoping she'll get to come home Tuesday. It looks like she may have a bronchoscopy on Monday to clear out her left lung and she'll have another echocardiogram at the same time, but if visual observation is any indication, she looks great to me. Even better, she says she can do without me for short periods of time.

And not soon enough. I'm not sure how much longer Lindsey can tolerate my not being home. I spent yesterday evening with Lauren and Lindsey and left Jessie on her own from around 7:30 p.m. to 1:15 a.m. I had planned to spend the night at home and return first thing in the morning, but left after Lindsey went to sleep and I finished some laundry.

I was concerned another lab tech would stop by and try to stick Jessie while I was gone. Sure enough, one stopped in some time after I returned, and I sent her on her way, asking her to send in the IV nurse instead.

All-in-all, I'm feeling much better about things.

* * *

<u>Sunday 3/19/06</u>
I just arrived back at the hospital after a restless night away. Lauren stayed over with Jessie, and I enjoyed a girls' night with Lindsey. We watched DVDs and did each other's hair, and I painted their nails. I know it didn't make up for all the time I've been away, but we both enjoyed it.

Lauren called sometime after 2:00 a.m. to ask about whether or not the lab techs were supposed to stick Jessie. I explained about the PTT being drawn by the IV nurses, but this was apparently ordered specifically to be compared to a sample from her central line to make sure her central line wasn't infected.

I never really made it back to sleep. I called the nurse after 3:00 a.m. to make sure Jessie was okay. She spiked a fever over 101, which I thought she'd been doing, but her records didn't show that, so I must have been mistaken.

The doctor ordered a new antibiotic, along with the blood and sputum cultures, so we're in another wait and see mode. I'm still hoping for a discharge early in the week. It seems to depend on this fever and what the cultures might show.

So, while I was up I updated my family and my writing group. I'm networked with an amazing group of women. They have certainly mobilized to leave care packages for my two younger kids while I'd moved into the hospital with Rain. They are looking after my young ones while I can't be there to do it myself.

It is an immeasurable comfort to me.

⋆ ⋆ ⋆

"Thanks, Mom, for staying here with me. I know it hasn't been easy for you." The hospital had settled into the quiet part of the night.

"Of course, Jess. I don't like it when you're here on your own."

She inhaled slowly. "So, I was thinking about this Viking burial—"

"Stop." I held up my hand. "I'm not talking to you about that, and I want you to quit thinking about it, okay?"

She frowned in frustration, but thankfully dropped the subject. "Other than that, then how are you holding up?"

"Me? I'm okay. I'd be better if you were all better and we could go home."

"Me, too."

"You'll get there," I said. "We just need to figure out this fever."

"I'll be happy when we can both get caught up on sleep," she said.

I nodded. "Speaking of sleep, I had a dream."

"What kind of dream?"

I told her about the three camels in the church and pulling the huge handfuls of pens and pencils from the one camel's mouth.

"That's weird," she said. "What does it mean?"

"Well, I found two meanings for camel that resonate with me." I held her gaze. "They were a long hard journey and great sadness."

Her gaze met mine. "It's about me, isn't it?"

I nodded. "I think so. I think the camels are three years, 2004, 2005 and 2006, the years you've been sick. And the mouth is expression. The pencils, pens and paintbrushes are self-explanatory."

Her gaze drifted away. "You're supposed to write about it." She looked back at me. "But not about 2004, at least you can't write it about me, though you should probably still write about it."

"Okay, if that's what you want."

"Yes, you can't write about me and that, but you should write about the rest."

"I will," I said. "Maybe it will help someone."

She nodded. "I'd like to think it will. There has to be some reason all of this is happening. Maybe if you write about it, it'll help someone else who might be going through something like this. Maybe that's why this is happening."

"Maybe. I think there's always a reason things happen. We may not understand what it is at the time, but I think that day will come when it's all clear to us."

"So, you'll write about it."

I nodded. "I've been journaling, but, yes, I think I'm supposed to write more beyond that."

She was silent a moment and then smiled. "Cool. So, will you read to me now?"

"Certainly."

* * *

Monday 3/20/06
We're still in the hospital. It seems that Jessie may have pneumonia again, a new occurrence not related to the one that brought us here. The energy and appetite she had Saturday have evaporated. She left her bed yesterday and so far today only to use the bedside commode, and that taxes her.

The dressing over her wound in her chest continues to leak as it is still draining. The ET nurses are working on it now. Phoenix, Christine and another friend of theirs stopped by earlier and I was surprised Jessie wanted visitors. She's normally protective of letting anyone see her when she's sick.

She's gotten so irate with me if I even mention calling her friends to let them know she's here.

A different pulmonologist was just by to see her. He talked about doing another bronch to wash out her left lung and possibly collect a sample of any mucus to culture. He also wants to take a small biopsy of her lung tissue to get some idea of what's going on in there.

Jessie wasn't too happy when he talked about the possibility of her lung collapsing in the process. It's a small chance, one to two percent, but she was concerned enough not to want to do the biopsy. I think it's a small enough risk and we should take the chance to get a better picture of what we're dealing with, but she refused to even consider it.

We've been here now for twenty-three days and we both long for home. I think a few good night's rest in her own bed will do Jess a lot of good, but with her hospital stay I'd put the basement renovation on hold and she said she wanted to move out of the basement and upstairs with the rest of us. Larry, Lauren and Lindsey have worked really hard to renovate the small upstairs bedroom for Lindsey, since they offered to move into what had been our guest room, freeing the big room for their sister.

I told them they could have their new room redone however they wanted. Larry had painted the walls white and replaced the old stained carpet with wood laminate. Lindsey is quite pleased, but we're not done yet.

I promised them as soon as I'm able we'll go shopping for window dressings, bedding and a canopy. I think it's important that they have that room exactly as they want it. Jessie is already looking forward to her new room.

We're still in the process, or Larry and the other kids are in the process, of clearing out the last of Lindsey's furniture and belongings so we can move Jessie's furniture upstairs. I won't ask Larry to do more, but if Jessie is discharged before we finish, we'll make her comfortable in the living room while Lauren and I move her bed.

Jessie is uncomfortable again with being left on her own in the hospital, so I remain with her and will continue to do so. It's still hard to be away from home. I miss Lauren and Lindsey, though Larry brings them to the hospital most days and I speak with them often. I can't wait to get Jessie home again.

CHAPTER TWELVE

The "H" Word

T<u>UESDAY 3/21/06</u>

Jessie still doesn't seem to be feeling better. She just turned away PT for the third day in a row, though she said she might feel up to it later. She hasn't eaten much of consequence in days. I've managed to get her to eat a bowl or two a day of Lipton's extra noodle soup, and she's always ready for hot chocolate.

The dietician brought us a sheet so we can record what Jessie eats and drinks. Nutrition is a valid concern. She is hungry though and has ordered off the alternate menu for lunch and dinner. Hopefully, we'll get her eating again and build her strength back up.

* * *

Wednesday 3/22/06

Hospice. _Mom volunteered with a hospice years ago. I remember her telling me about the great sadness of working with a couple and comforting the surviving spouse. My online friend Leslie, who I met through the Cancer Care support group, emailed about her husband spending time in the hospital, then moving to hospice care. I think it was just a matter of weeks before she emailed that he'd passed._

She has truly suffered in the aftermath of his death. She has poured her sorrow into her emails and my heart has gone out to her. I have emailed her some, but for much of the time my heart has been heavy with all the misery Jessie has faced. It seemed easier to disassociate for a time, because I didn't feel I could give Leslie the boost she needed. I'd been in such a dark place myself at times.

Then there was my conversation with Jessie's oncologist yesterday. I had asked him during his morning rounds when we could get Jessie home. Some of the other doctors have agreed that she was close to being ready to be discharged to home care, but yesterday was the first time anyone had used the H word.

Her oncologist slipped it in when we discussed her discharge. He said home hospice care would be good for her. I didn't think Jessie knew what he meant. She was just relieved to hear him say he'd work with the other doctors on a plan.

Shortly afterwards he caught me in the hall. He wanted to know where Jessie and I were at as far as discussing her impending future. He said he felt hospice care was appropriate for patients with a life expectancy of six months or less.

I told him Jessie could handle whatever he might have to say, reminding him we still had faith in the alternative treatment Solomon Wickey had advised. And I do have faith. Admittedly, a little more so since Jessie's bronch this afternoon. It's easier to visualize her recovery when I catch glimpses of her old self.

She called when I reached the hospital parking lot after picking up Lauren and Lindsey and dropping them at home. Jessie wanted Wendy's. I was thrilled that she seemed well enough to request food. She settled for Willy's and was confident enough that she was okay with me taking the time to stop by the drug store, as well.

When I returned she'd walked from the bathroom without her walker. She had no fever and her energy was at a good level. She seemed so much better, like she was on Saturday.

I had hoped we'd have a feverless night tonight, but that is not to be. Elizabeth, Jessie's night nurse, just gave her ibuprofen to lower her temp, which has been over 102 for hours with little relief, even after she'd taken acetaminophen.

At least she's sleeping. And though she's had her oxygen level increased, she's breathing without difficulty. I am counting our blessings. Tomorrow I'll see where we are in getting her home. We meet with the hospice people at 10:00 a.m.

* * *

I pushed through the door and stopped beside Jessie's bed. "Someone from the hospice will be here in a little bit."

"Okay. You'll be here, right?"

"Of course. I'm not going anywhere." I inhaled slowly. "Do you know what that is, honey?"

"Hospice?"

I nodded.

"It's like in-home care, right?"

"They have that, yes, and that is the kind of care you'll have."

"That's good. If you're going to need help, I want it to be a nurse."

"It will be, but do you know what hospice means?" I asked.

"What?"

"It means care for the terminally ill."

"Terminally ill." Her gaze locked on mine. "They consider me terminal? They're saying I'm dying."

As always, my denial remained firmly rooted. "Your doctors believe that, but I don't believe it. We haven't even started on the calcium and yucca, not to mention all of the other alternative treatments Marion researched for us. You have lots of options still."

She nodded slowly. "I didn't know that was what it meant."

I squeezed her hand. "They can believe whatever they want. We're not giving up. We haven't even started on the good stuff."

She nodded and offered me a half-hearted smile. "Can I start the calcium and yucca?"

"I'm still working with the doctors to get those added, though I think they may be close to okaying the calcium. We'll add the yucca and start you on the Essiac tea once we bust you out of here."

"Okay," she said. "Then let's get me out of here."

* * *

<u>*Thursday 3/23/06*</u>
We had a bit of excitement earlier when Jessie's blood pressure dropped and the nurse on duty called the rapid response team. Fortunately, we avoided a trip back to the CCU and they decided she just needed more fluids. She's resting now, though her temp's at 100.5.

We just spoke to a guy with the hospice service. He's getting paperwork ready. It seems we'll have whatever care Jessie needs to make her as comfortable as we can at home. I

135

had half hoped we'd have a nurse available every day to watch over her while I went back to work, but that doesn't seem to be the case.

Though Tom tells me to take what time I need and not worry about work, I do feel some self-imposed pressure to get back when I can. If Jessie continues to need someone with her twenty-four seven I will have to think about calling my sister Marion and asking her to come help for an indefinite period of time. I think she would have the most flexibility in her schedule.

I feel she'd come if I ask, but I wonder about the emotional impact. Jessie is so particular about who takes care of her and how they do it. I think she'd agree to Marion if she felt it was necessary, though.

I just don't know how much longer I can depend on donated vacation time. Not counting the month and a half to two months I took cumulatively during the transplant, I've been out for nearly a month with this hospital stay. If Jessie felt she could do without me, I'd go into the office for a few hours, but so far that hasn't been the case. As long as she needs me, I plan to be here for her.

So, I guess my focus is on getting her stable enough over the next few days to get her discharged. As soon as we're able, we'll start her on her calcium, yucca and Essiac and, hopefully, we'll see improvement.

For now, it seems she's back to where she was early yesterday, unable to get out of bed except to use the bedside commode and that's almost too taxing. At least we've managed to keep her out of CCU again.

* * *

We were fortunate to have a team of doctors working to get us out of the hospital and home. In that effort, they were sure to prepare us not only with the hospice home care we'd need, but with the knowledge of exactly what lay ahead for us.

Whenever I mentioned our plan to start her on alternative treatment, the medical team was sure to check me with as much reality as they thought I could bear.

On one such occasion her pulmonologist, the one who'd advised me to pray that first night she'd been intubated, turned to Jessie and me. "Do you want to know how this will go? How it will end?"

I glanced at Jessie. I think we both understood what he was asking. She nodded.

"As her lungs fail, which they will, it will become harder and harder for her to draw breath. She'll experience shortness of breath, rapid breathing, and it will feel like she just can't get enough air. She may start to panic. At that point we medicate her to make her as comfortable as possible. The medication will relax her and ease her way until her lungs cease to function."

Silence filled the room when he finished. I nodded. It was good to have him paint this picture, to prepare us for what he saw as inevitable, but even in light of this, my optimism held, or I suppose it was the denial I continued to hold onto. Whichever, I was resolved to get her home, get her strong enough to venture to the next therapy, be it oxygen treatment or working with a nutritionist on a thorough cleansing.

We'd get her home and we'd start anew.

* * *

At long last, towards the end of March, after twenty-eight days in the hospital, we arrived home on a Saturday afternoon. Jessie had been practicing climbing stairs during physical therapy in preparation for getting up to her new bedroom. My sister Maureen had insisted her husband, Lance, carry Jessie up the stairs. We'd appreciated their good intentions, but Jessie was determined to manage them on her own. I'd explained to my sister how particular Jess was about who could help her and that, if needed, Newt and I would be there to assist.

Now Jessie stood at the bottom of the stairs, one hand on the banister, her face turned up. I pasted on a smile and tried not to notice how her clothes hung off her.

"Whenever you're ready," I said. "Take your time. Newt and I are here for backup, but you've got this."

"All right." With a look of determination she pushed up first one step and then the next, continuing up the entire flight without stopping.

I followed immediately behind her as she hung a right at the top and headed into her new bedroom. Larry and the kids had brought up most of her furniture. We'd move the rest as we had time.

"I like it." Jessie smiled as she surveyed her new surroundings. She peered out the window facing the front of the house. "Lots of sunlight, just like I wanted."

"It can get hot in here in the summer."

"That's okay."

"Here's your bag," Newt said as she dropped the duffel on the bed. "Just let me know if you want anything else from the basement and I'll get it."

Jessie sank into her desk chair. I took it as a good sign that she didn't head straight for her bed. "I'm just going to sit here for a little bit. Lauren, is the computer hooked up?"

"It should be," Lauren said.

"If you're okay, I'm going to check on Lindsey," I said.

"Sure, I'm okay."

Lindsey had moved into their transformed new room, but had developed an unexplained fever that had lasted over a week. On our second visit to the pediatrician I'd asked about pneumonia. The doctor didn't think this could be the case, since they hadn't had any congestion or other symptoms that usually develop into pneumonia. But after I'd explained how they'd visited Jessie in the hospital while she had pneumonia they'd taken an X-ray of Lindsey's lungs and sure enough, they had pneumonia.

Poor thing had been feeling miserable for almost two weeks now. Even though Rain had already had this and was still recovering from the last bout, I thought it would be best if we kept the two of them as far apart as possible to prevent any further trading back and forth of the illness. So I'd invited Lindsey to camp out with me in my room at the other end of the hall.

"Hi, cutie," I said as I entered.

"Mom, I don't feel so good." Lindsey was huddled in my bed.

I dropped my own bag to feel their forehead. "When was the last time you had medicine?"

"I was just going to check their temperature," Newt said from the doorway. "They're due for another dose."

I nodded as I held the thermometer for Lindsey. They obediently opened their mouth and I inserted it under their tongue. I turned to Lauren. "Thanks for taking care of them, honey. What would I do without you?"

"Of course." Newt waved aside my question. "I'll see if Jessie's hungry. Can I get you guys anything to eat?"

Lindsey held up an empty water glass and I handed it to Newt. "I can make lunch."

"I've got it." She grinned. "We have lots of casseroles. You stay with Lindsey."

She may brush aside my gratitude, but Lauren was priceless. All my kids were priceless, of course, but I was so very fortunate to have Newt by my side, especially at times like these.

The thermometer beeped. "You are a little high, cutie."

I was able to spend some time with Lindsey and get their temperature down before the social worker arrived. She'd come to make sure we had everything in order for Jessie's hospice care. We sat in the living room while Lauren monitored her siblings upstairs.

"Now I know you don't want to think about this now, but the first thing you need to do is make arrangements," the woman said.

"Arrangements?" I said, dismay filling me. How could she come into my house and say this?

"Yes, funeral arrangements, arrangements for burial or cremation."

I pressed my lips together to keep from ordering her out the door. Of course she was well intended. She was just doing her job, but even though the doctors had given up on my daughter didn't mean that I had.

Denial was certainly a hard thing to shake.

"I know what you meant," I said, keeping my tone level. "I just think it's a little premature for that. As soon as my daughter is strong enough we're starting alternative treatments, and we've already begun with some new supplements that should help."

The woman's expression remained serious. "Certainly you should try whatever you feel will help Jessie, but you need to make those arrangements. If you don't do it now, it will be that much harder for you later. No one wants to deal with those details when they lose a loved one. It's better to have it all arranged."

I smiled tightly, resenting her school teacher tone. I'd make those arrangements when I was damn ready to and that time was not now.

* * *

"How are you doing?" I asked Jessie as I popped in to check on her later that evening.

"I have something I need to talk to you about."

Apprehensive, I sat on the bed beside her. After my talk with the social worker, I was in no mood to hear how she wanted a Viking burial. If she brought it up again, I'd have to cut her short. We were not going to plan a funeral, not on this day. I refused to give power to that line of thought.

I braced myself to stave off the conversation one more time. "What's up?"

"Well, you know how I signed the DNR?" she asked.

"Yes." She'd signed the Do Not Resuscitate order prior to her stem cell transplant.

"So there's no sense in me going back to the hospital. Besides I don't *want* to go back there."

"Yes," I said. "I don't want you to go back, either. I didn't think they were ever going to let you leave this last time." Where was she going with this?

"So I can't die here. If I die here you'll have to disclose it if you ever sell this house and it will ruin the property value. No one wants to buy a house where someone died."

If I hadn't been so upset by her ready acceptance of her death, I might have laughed, but by the look on her face Rain was completely serious.

"First of all," I said, "let's not be planning your death just yet."

"Check me into a hotel."

"What?" I stared at her in disbelief.

"When the time comes and I'm dying, check me into a hotel so you can maintain the value of your house."

"Are you kidding me?"

"I'm serious."

I turned to face her more directly. "If that time should come, you need to be where you're comfortable, with the people you love and who love you. You need to be home."

"But—"

"That's all we're going to say about that, miss." Before she could utter a rebuttal or bring up the Viking burial again, I left the room.

∗ ∗ ∗

The following day we had our first visit from the hospice nurse. After she checked Jessie's vitals, changed the dressing on her wound and then spent some time talking with Jessie, she pulled out a small white box.

"This is the E box." She opened the lid and pointed to the contents. "It has all the heavy hitting narcotics."

"What is that for?" Jessie asked.

"It's for keeping you comfortable at the end when things get rough. This will keep you calm." She handed me the box. "We'll talk about what to do with that when you need it."

I stared at the box.

The medication will relax her and ease her way until her lungs cease to function.

It was small for having such a big purpose. I set it on the nightstand. I'd think about that another time. I wasn't yet ready to contemplate the significance of having that box in my house.

CHAPTER THIRTEEN

A Loud Ring in the Night

LATE THE FOLLOWING EVENING, Jessie closed her eyes and leaned back against her pillows, breathing slowly and deliberately. She'd lost a good bit of weight during her hospital stay and she seemed so fragile in that moment.

I closed the book I'd been reading to her. "Do you want to sleep?"

She shook her head. "No, keep reading, please."

The doorbell sounded from below.

"Let me get you some tea."

Who could be visiting at this hour? I rose, as voices drifted up to us from downstairs. Newt met me at Jessie's bedroom door.

"Who's here?" Jessie asked.

Newt glanced at me before answering. "It's Jack, but I didn't let him in. I told him I'd have to check."

A sense of unease filled me. In spite of the fact that he and Rain had reconciled during her month at the extended stay hotel, Jack had been trouble the last I'd seen him.

"Let him in," Jessie said. "I want to see him."

"I don't know, Jess. I'll talk to him, but I don't think that's a good idea."

"Please, Mom, let him come up. I told you, we're cool."

My uneasiness grew as I headed down the stairs. I'd trusted this kid before and he'd betrayed that trust. I opened the front door. If Jack had come alone he may have had a chance, but he stood on the porch with another kid I'd never seen before. Back in the day, Rain had brought some bad characters to our house and we'd all suffered the consequences. I'd set a rule that no one was to bring strangers here without first clearing it with me.

Now Jack, who I already didn't trust, stood on my doorstep with a kid I didn't know, while Jessie struggled to regain her strength upstairs. Every motherly atom of my being rebelled at the idea of letting these guys into my house.

"I'm sorry, Jack, she's just not well enough for visitors."

"We won't stay long. We just want to say hello."

I glanced from him to his friend. "I don't think it's a good idea."

"Please, Mom," Rain called from upstairs, tears evident in her voice. "Let him come up."

Jack looked to me, his eyes imploring. "I promise I'll make it fast."

A quick gut check convinced me I couldn't budge on this. "No, Jack, I'm sorry. I'm not going to let you see her."

"Mom, please," Rain cried again, but I closed the door and bolted it. She could be upset with me for turning him away, but my instinct to keep them away from her had been too strong to deny.

* * *

Between Lindsey and Jessie I spent the next week or so running up and down the hall and then up and down the stairs as the hospice equipment arrived, an oxygen tank, a walker, a nebulizer. Jessie had refused a hospital bed.

Though she still wasn't up to leaving the house, she seemed stronger. She wasn't in a hurry to venture down the stairs again, but she was spending longer periods of time out of bed sitting at her desk.

The nurses had taken great care in showing me how to change the dressing on her chest wound. It was still draining and they'd shown me how to fashion a pouch over it that had to be emptied regularly. Since the hospice nurses didn't come every day, I spent a lot of time cleaning that wound, as well as staying on top of taking everyone's temperatures and administering whatever needed administering, be it meds or care.

Lindsey was still home struggling through her pneumonia one afternoon while Lauren was at school. I discovered Jessie's pouch was full and starting to leak. It had soaked through her shirt.

"I'm so sorry, honey. I should have checked this sooner."

"It's okay."

After slipping on the sterile gloves I wore while working with her wound, I removed the pouch. "Let me empty this and I'll be right back and we'll put on a fresh one and then clean you up and get you into fresh clothes," I said.

Worry filled me as I moved into the bathroom to discard the fluid. We hadn't seen an improvement yet with her taking the calcium, yucca and Essiac and until she had the strength to navigate the stairs again, there would be no oxygen therapy. I inhaled slowly, feeling depleted as I struggled to open the pouch.

Something hit against the side of the clear plastic. I raised the pouch, peering at what appeared to be some kind of bodily tissue, about an inch in diameter, with an irregular outline, floating in the fluid. I stared in shock.

Was it tissue from Jessie's lung?

"Mom," Lindsey called from down the hall.

"Hold on, cutie. I'll be there in a sec." It was times like these that I missed Newt being home during the day.

"Mom!"

The urgency in Lindsey's voice had me yanking on the pouch's opening. The liquid missed the toilet and splattered all over me and the bathroom. I hate to admit I was a little horrified as it seeped into my shirt.

I had no time to contemplate whatever had been in the pouch. The muffled sounds of my poor Lindsey throwing up drifted to me from down the hall.

I raised my eyes heavenward. "Uncle."

After discarding the pouch and gloves I hurried to them in my fluid soaked clothes, leaving the bathroom to deal with when I could get back to it.

"I'm so sorry," they said miserably. Vomit covered them and my bed.

I resisted the urge to sink to my knees and cry. I couldn't even hug them, for fear of contaminating them with whatever I'd spilled on myself. Instead, I tossed them a towel.

"No worries, sweet one. I'll be right back."

* * *

Somehow, we made it through that particularly low point. Lindsey got better just in time for spring break, which hit the first week of April. Though Jessie still hadn't made it downstairs, she spent a couple of days at her computer. She was using her oxygen less. It seemed she was rallying.

With Lauren home for the break I felt it would be safe to run into the office for a few hours. It was less than ten miles from home and I could hurry back if needed. I spent about three hours at work that Monday, calling regularly to check in. Jessie actually made it downstairs, without use of her walker. She sat in the kitchen with Lauren for much of the afternoon, watching her sister bake a pie.

Heartened, I ventured into work again on Tuesday. I'd been there for two hours when I called to check to see how all was going at home.

"How is she?" I asked when I had Newt on the phone.

"She's coughing up blood."

Concern filled me. "I'm on my way."

I called the hospice nurse while en route. Before Jessie's last bronchoscopy, the doctor ordered a dose of vitamin K to counter her blood thinner. I'd been shocked when the hospice nurse had provided the new dosage for her blood thinner post-discharge. I'd even had her double check with the doctor. Thinking back, I don't know why we didn't have Jessie's portacath removed when her central line was removed. If we had, she wouldn't have needed the blood thinner.

Regardless, I'd latched onto the theory that her blood thinner dosage was too high. This had to be why she was coughing up blood. In my usual state of denial, I had to pin it on something. That way, I could develop an action plan to fix the problem. It gave me something concrete to do.

I rushed to Jessie's side when I reached home. She was in bed. The blood had already begun staining her lips. I dabbed at it with a tissue to no avail.

"Not feeling so hot today?" I asked.

Tears gathered in her eyes and glinted off her pale cheeks. "I'm sorry, Mom. I've been putting up a good front. I didn't want you to worry, but the truth is my lungs aren't getting any better."

I glanced at the oxygen tank on the other side of her bed. Against my urgings, she'd been opting not to use it. "Let me get your oxygen."

She shook her head. "It won't matter." More tears seeped out of the corners of her eyes. "I didn't sleep last night. Every time I fell asleep, I'd stop breathing. I have to focus now to make my lungs work."

"The hospice nurse is coming. I asked her again about your blood thinner. Maybe you should eat something with vitamin K."

She shook her head. "I'm not hungry."

It seemed to take forever for the hospice nurse to arrive. She looked over Jessie and then turned to me, holding out her hand, palm up. "Do you have the E box?"

I stared at her hand a moment. So deep was my denial at that point that as I handed her the E box I thought, So it isn't just for the end. It will get her through this rough patch and then we can get it replenished for when she really needs it.

The nurse gave me new instructions, adding the hard narcotics to Jessie's medication regimen. I kept track by logging everything in a notebook.

After the nurse left, I sat on the bed beside Jessie. She was unusually pale.

"Here, honey, let me see if I can clean you up a little."

I wiped her lips with a wet washcloth this time, but still made no improvement in removing the blood. Not wanting to cause her anxiety by pointing out the stain, I set aside the washcloth. Her cough had become frequent. Each bout seemed to weaken her more.

I didn't mention the E box, even though we'd discussed it in front of her. "The nurse brought cough medicine and vitamin K. That should help."

"Please stay with me," Jessie said. "Don't let me sleep."

"I'm not going anywhere. Do you want me to read to you?"

She shook her head. "I have to concentrate."

My throat tightened. "Okay."

"Reiki me, please."

I slid down beside her and placed my hands on her back.

"Thank you," she said, relaxing a little. "It's all that helps now."

"No worries, honey. I'm here."

I called in the angels and anchored myself to my oversoul and then grounded into the earth before filling my heart with my love for my child and pouring it into her. And then I called in the Reiki.

The hours stretched on, broken up by medication dosages as she drifted in and out of consciousness. When she dozed I remained alert. I was exhausted, though, and drifted off at some point, my hands on her back, monitoring each inhale and exhale.

Wednesday, April fifth, dawned and we continued the regimen. I kept encouraging her to eat, still wanting to get more vitamin K into her system. I left her for only the briefest trips to the bathroom.

At some point late that night, I thought of Mommy Cat. She'd been Larry's cat and her real name had been Chanelle, but because she'd had a kitten when we met, she was always Mommy Cat to me. Mommy Cat remained with us for many years. I'm not sure how old she was, but all the hairs on her chin had grayed. She'd lived a good life. I spent Mommy Cat's last night on this earth sitting with her on our back patio.

I'd known then she was dying and as the soft light on Rain's nightstand illuminated her in the stillness of how she lay, in her struggle to draw each breath, I couldn't help but think of Mommy Cat and her last night. Only in that moment did I let go of my denial as it dawned on me that Jessie, too, was really leaving us.

I wept quietly as I finally accepted the inevitable.

She rolled toward me, her words halting. "I'm sorry...I can't get all...emotional...with you. I'm fighting...to breathe."

"It's okay, honey." I inhaled slowly before continuing. "Do you remember when you were in the hospital and you told me that the only reason you were still here was because of me and I told you that I was going to keep holding on tightly as long as you needed me to?" My throat burned, but I forced out the words as I blinked through my tears. "I'm not holding on anymore. I'm letting go."

She responded only by rolling again to her side, her back to me. I kept my hands on her, continuing to monitor each inhale and exhale. I briefly considered calling family and friends, but for the most part Jessie had been adamantly against people seeing her when she was sick. I closed my eyes as a vision of her colorless features and blood-stained lips floated before me. She wouldn't want this to be everyone's last memory of her.

Should I wake Lauren and Lindsey, though? Again, I didn't think Jessie would want this to be their last memory of her. It was better for everyone to remember her when she'd been stronger.

She continued to drift in and out after that. At one point she was coherent enough for us to try the nebulizer, but we hadn't had room for it upstairs, so I'd left it in the basement. Not wanting to wake Lauren, I dashed downstairs as quickly as I could.

"Can you sit?" I asked Jessie after I'd returned and gotten it ready with the medication.

We got her into a half-sitting position and then I helped her place the plastic mask over her nose and mouth. She struggled with maybe two short breaths, before shaking her head.

She pulled the mask from her face, saying, "No, I can't take it."

My heart sank. I couldn't get her to use the oxygen, and now the nebulizer had failed her. We were truly out of options at this point. I set aside the nebulizer and lay beside her once more. Again I prayed.

Then sometime just after two in the morning she sat straight up in the bed, wide awake and alert. "Maybe I *should* eat something."

My heart leapt. She had an appetite. This was music to my ears. Excited, I grabbed a nearby tray with a bowl of cereal on it that I'd tried to get her to eat earlier. She was still sitting up as I turned with the tray.

"Do you want milk with the cereal?" I asked.

"Yes, milk would be good."

I set the tray on the bed near her and raced to the door. Not wanting to leave Rain's side, I called down the hall for Lauren, waking her.

She hurried to her sister's room, stopping in to see Jessie sitting up and fully conscious. "Is everything okay?"

"She's hungry," I said, smiling. I pointed to the bowl of cereal. "Can you please get her some milk?"

As Newt hurried off I turned back to Jessie. "I'm so glad you're hungry. This is a good sign."

Newt returned in a flash and handed me the milk, before retreating again to her room. I poured the milk into Jessie's cereal, and then turned to her, spoon in hand.

She wobbled. "I...can't..." Her grip was clumsy as she grabbed one of her pillows and maneuvered it beside her, trying to stack it on top of another pillow to support herself as she tottered.

I frowned at the spoon in my hand, my sleep deprived, denial-filled mind locking only on the fact that she was having trouble grabbing the pillow. "How are you going to use a spoon?"

She isn't going to eat.

The thought barely escaped my mind before she started to collapse. I dropped the spoon and lunged forward as I yelled for Newt.

"I can't see," Jessie said.

Reaching out, I caught her as she fell backward. I managed to angle her fall so her head just missed hitting the wall.

"Call 911." Lauren moved into the room, her expression stricken. She settled on the bed beside us.

"It's too late," I said.

"We can try."

"She had a DNR. She didn't want that."

I tried to pull Jessie further down the bed to straighten her out, but she was a limp handful for me. She lay with her neck at a slight angle, the top of her head against the wall where we hadn't yet gotten her a headboard. She drew one ragged breath, her chest moving upward as her eyes stared blankly at the ceiling. I held my own breath as her chest rose and then fell one last time.

And then my sweet girl was gone.

"Jessie?" Her face blurred before me and tears rolled down my cheeks. I folded over her and wept.

When I could compose myself, I gently closed her eyes and then moved to Lauren's side. I wrapped my arms around her while we both cried. Eventually, I pulled back and inhaled slowly.

"Should we wake Lindsey?" Lauren asked.

"Let's let them sleep. I'll tell them in the morning." I gestured to Jessie's body. "I'm going to wash the blood off her lips, clean her up a little."

Newt wiped her eyes. "I'll shave her legs. She'd want that."

We worked together in the deep quiet of the wee morning hours. After cleaning Jessie's lips and mouth, I washed her hair as Newt shaved her sister's legs, the gentle splash of the water and the scrape of the razor the only sounds to stir the night.

Then suddenly, the landline rang once, ripping through the quiet, startling us both.

As the silence again folded over us, I looked at Lauren. "Do you think that was Jessie?"

She nodded slowly. "Yes. I think she's telling us she's okay."

I gave her a small smile. "Yes, I think you're right."

CHAPTER FOURTEEN

How to Plan a Viking Burial?

I DIDN'T SLEEP FOR THE FEW REMAINING hours until dawn, when I gently woke Lindsey. "Honey, I'm so sorry, but I have something to tell you."

They sat up beside me, rubbing their eyes. "Is it Jessie?"

"Yes." I paused, not quite able to say the words. I inhaled a shaky breath. "She passed early this morning."

"She died?"

My throat tightened. "Yes, honey."

They nodded and bowed their head. I pulled them to my side and hugged them. They'd drawn a picture for Jessie earlier in the week with a note saying they hoped she felt better. Even though they hadn't gotten along, it still had to hurt to lose their sister.

* * *

Not long after, I sat at the computer, looking up funeral homes. Of course, I hadn't heeded the social worker's advice to make plans in advance. My eyes felt like sandpaper.

"Mom, you know what we have to do."

I stared at Lauren, groaning inwardly. *The Viking burial.* "I never let her talk to me about it. I cut her off every time. I don't really know what she wanted, or how the hell I would manage such a thing."

"I talked to her about it. She told me what she wanted. Mom, we have to try."

"I wouldn't know where to start." I turned back to the computer. Where did one begin when planning a Viking burial for one's deceased child? I couldn't think about that now. I had to find a funeral home.

A short while later, Lauren returned and held out a slip of paper. I stared at it a long moment. Slowly, I took it from her, the words and numbers puncturing the numbness blanketing my mind.

"Mom, you know you have to try. You said you didn't know where to start. I thought this might be a good place."

Surprise filled me as I stared at the slip, "Natural Resources Permitting Office?"

Newt shrugged. "I'm thinking maybe we could try the lake."

God, what a nightmare. Every time Rain had mentioned the burial—the open cremation at sea—I had changed the subject. How could I discuss such a thing with my nineteen-year-old daughter?

It was unthinkable.

But at 2:24 that morning, in the quiet comfort of our home, the unthinkable had happened. Jessie had lost her battle with cancer, or whatever had ailed her.

"I don't know, honey." I shook my head and tamped down on the grief threatening to claim me. I couldn't lose it now. I had to get through this. I had to make plans.

"Mom." A note of censure tinged Newt's voice. She'd matured way beyond her almost seventeen years. "We have to try. *I'll* call."

"You think we can get a permit to have a Viking burial on Lake Lanier?"

Newt shrugged again. "I don't know. It seemed like a reasonable option."

Shit. As she left my heart pounded. I pressed the numbers on my cell's keypad. A man's clipped voice answered, and I closed my eyes. "I...I don't know who to ask, so maybe you can help direct me."

"Yes, ma'am, I'm happy to try," he said.

"My daughter, my nineteen-year-old daughter—" my voice cracked. I drew a deep breath, and then blundered on. "She..." *Shit. Shit. How to say it?* "She passed away this morning, and she wanted a Viking burial."

"Oh, I'm so sorry for your loss, ma'am. You said a Viking burial?"

"You know, her body in a small boat and we set it on fire..."

"Right, yes."

I bit my lip. "An open cremation at sea, only since we're inland, my other daughter thought maybe we could do it on Lake Lanier, that maybe we could get a permit for it."

A short silence buzzed across the line. "Well, uh, I really don't know. No one's ever asked us that before. Maybe you should try the Georgia Wildlife Law Enforcement Division. They handle things from an enforcement perspective. Maybe they'd know if it's okay."

"I see. Thank you, I'll try them."

He gave me the number, which I dialed next. Again, I told the man who answered why I'd called. "I tried the Natural Resources Permitting office, but they suggested I ask you."

A short silence hummed across the line. "Well, I don't know, ma'am. No one's ever asked us that. Maybe you should try the environmental protection department. If anyone has a problem with it, it would be them. Maybe they can give you some kind of clearance."

"I see, of course. Thank you, I'll give them a call."

After he gave me the number, I hung up. I had so many other calls to make: the rest of my family, Rain's friends. I closed my eyes again. God, how could I tell Jessie's friends? Most of them didn't even know she'd been hospitalized this last time, since she'd been adamant about not calling them. I understood that she hadn't wanted them to see her so ill, but they were going to be blindsided by this.

Pushing aside a new wave of grief, I dialed the next number. I had to figure out this Viking burial thing. Newt was right. We had to at least make every effort.

A young woman answered. "State of Georgia Department of Environmental Protection."

"Is this the director's office?" I asked.

"Yes, it is. Was there something I could help you with?"

"Is he in?"

"I'm sorry; he's on his other line. Would you like to leave a message?"

I drew a deep breath. "Maybe you can help." I explained my reason for calling. "I spoke to the Department of Natural Resources Permitting Office and then their law enforcement division, and they directed me to you."

"I'm so sorry for your loss, ma'am. I don't think there's anything we can do, though. I've never heard of such a thing. I'm guessing the danger as far as an environmental concern would be if the fire didn't burn everything..."

My stomach turned. "That's okay; I didn't think we'd be able to. I just...had to try. Thank you so much for your time."

"Wait, he's off. Would you mind holding and I'll see if he's available?"

"I'll hold, thank you."

After a short while she came back on the line. "Hello?"

I gripped the phone. "Yes?"

"I think we can help you. You should be able to do this if you go off the coast beyond any area of jurisdiction."

"Really?" A sense of relief filled me. "I have a brother in Savannah. We could go somewhere off the coast there. Would that work?"

"It should. You don't need to make any more calls. We'll start with the Secretary of State's office and clear this through whatever agencies needed. I'll get back to you with exact coordinates off the coast near Savannah."

The room blurred and my throat again tightened. "Thank you so much. I can't tell you how much this means to us."

"You're welcome. We're so sorry, ma'am," the assistant said. "We're going to do what we can to help. You'll hear from me shortly."

After giving the woman my number and thanking her again, I disconnected and found Newt. "It looks like we may have a Viking burial after all, at least Rain's version."

Newt nodded. "She wanted archers with flaming arrows."

"I know, but where are we going to find that? Maybe my brother knows someone. I guess I can Google archers in Savannah. Maybe there's a club or something."

Ten minutes later the director's assistant at the Environmental Protection Department called again. "I'm so sorry, but I have some bad news," she said. "We talked to our attorneys and they said there are statutes against open cremations like that."

"I see." My heart sank. "Well, thank you for trying. I really appreciate your help."

"I'm so sorry, ma'am."

"We gave it our best shot," I said, my throat tight. "You've been most helpful."

After I hung up I explained to Newt. "I'm sorry, honey."

"It's okay, Mom."

"We'll get a model of a Viking ship and put her ashes in it and light it on fire," I said. "But it'll have to be separate from the memorial service."

"Yes, and she had a very specific guest list." Newt ran through a short list of Rain's closest friends and family. "That's it. No one else."

"She didn't want the rest of my family?"

"No."

I pinched the bridge of my nose. How would I tell them? At the same time I understood Jessie's reasoning. She only wanted those who were the closest to her at her funeral. Hopefully, my family wouldn't have trouble accepting it.

"So, she planned the guest list, but did she mention where she wanted this to take place?"

"Sorry, Mom, we never discussed where."

"Well, I guess that'll be the first thing we'll need to figure out then," I said.

Beyond exhausted, I dropped my head into my hands. I'd wait until after the weekend to work that one out, because as of now I didn't have a clue. Before I could even think about where Jessie would want the ash ceremony, I had to finish my phone calls.

* * *

A couple of hours later we sat in the living room with Larry, Maureen, her husband, Lance, and Freddy, another family friend, who came to sit in vigil with us while we waited for the hospice nurse to arrive. I'd called first thing that morning, but by eleven the nurse still hadn't gotten there, not that she needed to hurry at this point.

Sometime midmorning I stepped into Jessie's room and frowned. I'd raised all the blinds to let in as much sunshine as I could, since that had been her main reason for moving upstairs. Someone had lowered them, though I'm sure whoever did it only meant to show respect and hadn't realized I'd opened them on purpose. I couldn't abide having my girl in the dark, though.

Lots of sunlight, just like I wanted.

With quick movements, I drew up the blinds and again let in the sunshine, so it shone over Rain's still form on the bed. I stood for a moment beside her, torn between staying and returning to our guests. But my sweet girl was no longer there, so, satisfied her body was getting the sunlight she'd wanted, I descended the stairs once more to sit with my family as we continued to wait for the nurse.

The nurse arrived at some point in the afternoon and at long last I stood with her in Jessie's bedroom. The nurse turned to me. "Why didn't you call us when it happened?"

"I didn't see the point. It was in the middle of the night. You couldn't have done anything." And I hadn't wanted a lot of commotion at that time. The peace had been a blessing.

She nodded and then held my gaze. "Did anything...unusual happen?"

"As a matter of fact, it was kind of odd." I explained about Jessie sitting up and saying she should eat and Lauren's delivering the milk, then again retiring, only to rush back when I again called for her in time to witness her sister's last breaths.

The nurse again nodded. "She was already leaving her body. Her suffering eased and she rallied at the end. I hear stories like this all the time."

She collected the remaining drugs from the E box. "Have you called the funeral home?"

"Yes, they said they couldn't come until after you got here. I'll call them to let them know you're finished."

⋆ ⋆ ⋆

"Ma'am, I'm so sorry, but could I have a word with you?" one of the men from the funeral home asked later that afternoon.

160

"Sure." I glanced around at the small gathering of people in our living room. "I'll be right back."

"I hate to have to tell you this," he said quietly. "But the angle of the stairs won't accommodate the stretcher. We've tried several different ways, but we can't get it to work."

I stared at him.

"We're going to have to carry her down."

"Oh," I said. "Okay."

He cleared his throat. "She's already...it might look a little..." He glanced beyond me to Lindsey and the rest of the people gathered in our living room. "I don't think it's anything you'd want to see. We don't want to distress anyone."

"Of course." I gestured to Lindsey. "I'll take my youngest to the back bedroom with me, and I'll warn the others."

"Yes, ma'am, thank you. I think that would be best."

What seemed an eternity from when my dear Jessie had left us, we followed the hearse carrying her body to the funeral home. With Larry, my sister and brother-in-law, we formed a small procession as we headed through the streets of Roswell.

The funeral home director met us as we entered the facility. The kids stayed with their aunt and uncle while Larry and I met with the man in his office.

"Do you know what kind of plans you'd like to make?" the director asked.

"She wanted to be cremated," I said. "And we'd like to hold a memorial service."

"Let me show you the chapel. It would be a nice place for you to hold the service. And then you can choose an urn."

The rest of our party followed as he led us into the chapel. A large cross hung at the front, pews adorned the center and stained glass windows lined the walls. In unison, we shook our heads.

"It's lovely," I said to the director. "But she really wasn't a church kind of girl. What else do you have?"

He frowned. "Well, I do have a couple of viewing rooms. They aren't as big, but they're connected and we can open up the dividing wall to make it one big room."

The space was small, but would do. I'd be sure to limit the number of my friends I invited, so we could accommodate more of Jessie's friends.

"You could have the casket up front if you want to have a viewing." The director gestured toward an area at one end.

"No," I said. "She wouldn't want that." If she hadn't wanted her friends to see her when she was sick, she surely wouldn't want them to see her now.

"Well, then you'll have more room. We can set up more rows of chairs and you can have a table there for pictures, then," he said.

My sister nodded. "I'd like to help with pictures."

"Thanks," I said. "That would be nice." I turned to the funeral home director. "Could we see what you have for her ashes?"

We chose a polished box of blond wood with rounded corners for her ashes. Maureen stepped beside me. "Is that the one you want? Please let me get that for you."

I nodded. She was grieving nearly as much as I was. "Thank you."

The director showed us the panel at the bottom. "It slides out and makes it easier to spread the ashes, if that's what you want to do."

I glanced at Lauren. "We'll have to figure all of that out."

After we finished planning the details, the director straightened. "If you could drop off the clothes you'd like her to wear in the morning we'll do the cremation tomorrow. Since you aren't having a viewing, we can get that done earlier and then you can have the memorial service Saturday evening."

Again, I turned to Newt. "Would you like to pick out her outfit?"

Her lips curved into a small smile. "Yes, I know exactly what she'd like to wear."

"Good." The director gestured toward a back room. "They have her ready if any of you would like to say a last goodbye, then."

We followed him down a short hallway to stand outside of a back room. We went in one at a time, except for Lindsey.

"I don't want to go in there," they said while Newt was saying her goodbyes.

"You don't have to, sweetie. It's okay."

Rain was no longer in the body that lay coldly in that back room. Still, when it had been my turn I'd taken the opportunity to touch her cheek and memorize the curve of her chin one last time. I didn't really feel the need to say goodbye, though.

My Jessie would always be with me.

CHAPTER FIFTEEN

Not a Church Girl

Eᴀʀʟʏ ᴛʜᴇ ɴᴇxᴛ ᴍᴏʀɴɪɴɢ ᴀɴ unearthly stillness startled me awake. A storm had moved into our area, but had temporarily abated. I lay for a moment, my ears straining in the silence. No scrape of tires sounded in the distance, no birdsong drifted in from outside and not a soul stirred in the house.

With heart-wrenching clarity, the events of the previous day crowded in on me: the endless night with Jessie, her last breath, washing her hair while Newt shaved her legs, waiting for hours for first the hospice nurse, then the people from the mortuary, the calls to friends and family. God, that had been a disaster. I had blurted the news to one too many shocked receivers, until Newt had taken over the task.

I understood shock. Rain had been vital and strong just days before. I closed my eyes, trying to shut out the memories. Jessie was gone, truly gone. The realization hit again with striking force. I crumpled against the mattress, my tears coming hard and fast, my breath ragged, the pain unbearable. I turned my face to my pillow, muffling my sorrow in order not to wake the kids.

For long moments, I lay in twisted torment. Then because I must, because I had no choice, I dragged myself into the shower. Hot water sprayed over me, sobs spilling from me in incoherent spasms.

By the time I dried and dressed, my crying jag had ended. I'd pushed the worst of my grief deep inside, to deal with later. My head pounded, but I had much to take care of.

My conversation with Newt over the Viking burial rounded in my mind. I closed my eyes.

Jessie, honey, I'm sorry we couldn't do the Viking burial the way you wanted. We tried. We did. But we'll do our own version with your ashes. Just tell me where you want us to do the ceremony. I'm sorry I wouldn't discuss it with you. I couldn't, not then, but now I need to know. Give me a sign, something. I need to know where you want your ashes.

I sat quietly for a moment, listening for anything—the whisper of a thought—but nothing came to me. Thunder boomed in the distance. I shook myself. The rest of my family would be arriving today. I needed to get groceries. Lauren and I had to take Jessie's clothes to the mortuary.

Newt had picked out Rain's cremation outfit, her favorite jeans, rainbow socks and the T-shirt Newt had made her when Rain had gotten sick and suddenly everyone wanted to hug her, comfort her. Jessie had hated it. Across the front of the shirt Newt screen printed the words, "I REQUIRE 3 FEET OF PERSONAL SPACE SO BACK THE F*#K UP."

I had actually smiled when Newt chose the top. They'd scheduled the cremation for this afternoon, before tomorrow's service. I stuck by my decision that Jessie would have wanted it that way. To have a viewing at her memorial service wasn't an option.

A soft knock sounded at my door. I glanced in my mirror, despaired over my red nose and eyes, then opened the door to Lauren.

"There's a woman here." Newt peered at me. "She says she's here to clean the house."

I nodded. "Yes, Patti arranged it." My dear writing buddies continued to provide their support. Patti Henry had arranged for the cleaning before Rain's passing, but I'd told her I didn't want to cancel. I had a house full of people on the way.

"I can ask her to come back."

"No, honey, I'll come down." I moved past Lauren then turned again toward her. "Are you okay?"

She nodded. Tough as nails and steady as they come was my second born. I gave her a small smile, and then pulled her into a quick hug.

"Thanks for being there for me yesterday, Newt, yesterday and always. I couldn't have gotten through any of it without you."

"You would have managed."

"Not as well. These past couple of years have been hard on all of us, but sometimes I wonder if I asked too much of you."

"I'm fine, Mom. I'm the last one you need to worry about." She gave me a small smile.

"You've had to grow up so fast."

I didn't wait for a response. I turned, then headed past Lindsey's closed door to the stairs and the waiting housekeeper below. The woman was from South America and had a ready smile. She held a bucket filled with cleaning supplies.

"Thank you for coming," I greeted her. "We anticipate a full house."

She nodded, her gaze solemn, her accent heavy as she said, "I'm sorry to hear about your daughter. My condolences."

"Thank you."

I glanced at the closed door to Rain's room at the top of the stairs. "If you would, please leave that first bedroom on the right alone. I'll take care of it myself."

"Of course." The woman stuck out her hand. "I'm Rosalea."

I shook her hand, saying, "I'm Dorene. It's nice to meet you."

"I'd like to start upstairs, if that's okay."

"Of course. You can begin in my room. Left at the top and all the way down on the right."

The woman nodded, and then moved up the stairs. I followed as far as Lindsey's room. Their door stood slightly ajar. Newt sat on the bed beside her sibling. "You don't have to wear black. You can wear whatever you want. Rain wouldn't care."

Lindsey nodded, frowning. "I'm not getting up and saying anything."

"No, you don't have to, unless you want to."

"It's not like I have any happy memories of her."

My heart constricted at Lindsey's matter-of-fact statement. Jessie had liked to dish it out, but few tossed it right back at her the way Lindsey had.

For a moment longer, I hesitated outside the door, debating entering. In the end I headed to the kitchen to make breakfast. As always, Newt had Lindsey well in hand. Where Jessie had been Lindsey's nemesis, Lauren had been their champion and somehow she'd managed to stay in Jessie's good graces anyway. Such was her diplomatic nature.

Forty-five minutes later, the kids sat idly chatting over the remnants of the eggs and toast I had scraped together. I moved into the adjoining living room in search of glasses for the dishwasher. Rosalea was there dusting.

She turned to me. "May I ask you a question?"

"Sure."

"Do you believe in, how you say..." She pressed her hand to her forehead. "Premonitions?"

"I do, yes."

She smiled shyly. "Before your friend called, God—" She stopped and gestured with her hands. "He talks to me—"

"Yes?" Filled with curiosity, I encouraged her to continue.

"And He told me I would come here. So I knew even before she called me what she would ask and that I would be coming here to you. I knew only that I had a purpose in coming, but not what that purpose would be. And so when she did call, I smiled and agreed right away to come."

A shiver ran up my arms. "And do you know what that purpose is now?"

"I think I am to give you a message...from Him." She cocked her head. "She is okay—your daughter. She was always an angel, even though you might not have thought so, and He needed her more than you did."

My throat tightened. The room blurred. "I know."

"He tells me. And there's more." She gestured to the sofa. "Please sit."

We sat and she told me many wonderful things, finishing with, "And you have to believe in Him."

I felt a little like I was being chastised. I was more spiritual than religious, but I believed in God. I might not show it every day, but growing up Catholic, that belief had been pretty well ingrained.

Still, could it be true? Could this woman, who'd come to clean my house, actually have messages from God, or as Rain would have said, Spirit? Whatever the reality was around Rosalea's visit, my conversation with her lifted my grief in a way nothing else would or could have. Somehow, I was able to move forward with a lighter heart.

* * *

April 6, 2006, saw a major outbreak of severe weather throughout the southeast, lasting for three days and spawning thunderstorms in Fulton County, Georgia. The storm uprooted trees, knocked down power lines and destroyed buildings in Roswell. Thunder shook the ground and rain poured down in torrents, slashing through the trees and pelting the roof as I tossed in my bed the night of Rosalea's visit.

The following morning, I awoke to the steady drum of rain overhead and on the leaves outside my window. As thunder boomed in the distance thoughts of Jessie filled me. This was her element. To me, it was a sign that she was with us still.

Nearly two years later, these same thoughts would return to me when we lost my mother. I pushed through the wind as I walked into the church where we held Mom's funeral, the rain slashing sideways with such force that I was soaked in spite of my umbrella. Once inside, I stood near enough to one of my brothers to overhear as he spoke to the priest.

"We'll have it moved right away," the priest said.

"Thank you." My brother shook his hand.

I glanced past them to my mother's coffin. It rested below an evident weak spot in the church's roof. Rain dripped down from the high ceiling, splattering across the polished wood of the closed lid.

It was raining on my mother's coffin. Chills ran up my arms and I smiled. I had no doubt Rain was telling me she was with her grandmother.

The rainy morning of Jessie's memorial service I turned on the news as I dressed. Many areas of Roswell and the surrounding cities had lost power during the storm. At least our neighborhood hadn't been affected, though with all of the trees in my yard I'd need to check for damage from falling limbs.

I called the funeral home, waiting impatiently until someone answered. "Hi, I just wanted make sure you're open and didn't have any damage from the storm."

"We're here, we're open and thankfully, we didn't have any damage."

"Great," I said. "I'll see you tonight, then."

* * *

"I met Rain twice." Smiling, the petite brunette standing at the front of the mortuary's viewing room held up two fingers. "And she was awesome, so awesome that when I heard what had happened, though I was completely booked, I cancelled everything just so I could be here tonight. There just isn't any place else I'd rather be."

From my seat at the front, I glanced around the two adjoining viewing rooms. I could think of a million other places I'd rather be besides at a memorial service for my first born. But the memorial service was a necessary part of passing Rain. So we'd crowded into these two connected viewing rooms. The combined area was maybe one third the size of the chapel and it filled up that night. Jessie's friends had come en masse, friends I had previously met and ones I saw for the first time that evening.

The brunette now sharing her story at the front of the room was one of the latter. She continued, "I was just hanging out one night and I looked over and I saw these two girls. It was Rain and Newt and I thought, 'they look cool and I want to meet them.'" Her smile widened. "And so I ran up to Rain and I humped her leg."

As her words registered, Newt sprang forward from her front row seat. The girl straddled her leg. She gave two quick thrusts of her hips before stepping back, grinning, leaving no doubt as to her meaning.

I stared for a moment, taken aback, and then I stifled a smile. Jessie would have loved it.

"And I knew when Rain went right along with it that we'd be friends." As the brunette told of her brief friendship with Jessie, I stole a glance at my mother.

Confusion marred her expression, but I couldn't mistake the offended looks on others in the audience. I think if they had understood Jessie, the story wouldn't have bothered them.

I sighed and turned my attention back to the front, where my nephew Nick had stepped forward. "I thought I'd picked a really good hiding spot," he said. "But after a while I figured out that she wasn't even looking for me."

Laughter rippled through the room, hopefully distracting them all from the humping story. After he returned to his seat, another of Rain's friends read a poem, then more memory sharing followed.

Probably the best part of the memorial was closer to the start, though, after I'd said my piece and then invited everyone to share their stories. My sweet Lauren stood before us and set the tone for the rest with a good dose of honesty.

"For starters, Rain would've laughed at this room and made that eww face," she said. "So just keep in mind that this place doesn't represent her in the least bit. Now, some of you knew Rain as a sister, a niece, a cousin, a friend, a daughter or a granddaughter. But all of you who knew her well knew that she wasn't a perfect angel. Normally at these things, only the good side of a person is described. Bad qualities are left out in an attempt to leave memories of a falsely better person. I don't think we should do that here. All of her 'flaws' were a part of her, and a part of why we loved her.

"For example, she was extraordinarily vulgar and liked being called an asshole. She was also highly racist. Pyke can vouch for that.

"Everyone remember that hacking thing she did? Well, sometimes when she hacked up a major loogie and didn't want to get up, she'd spit it into whatever container was closest, which just so happened to be my water glass most of the time. It was terribly gross when I didn't notice until it was too late.

"She would also show everybody when she hacked up something particularly interesting. 'Look, there's some green and orange in this one.' She was doing that just a few days ago, when some really strange looking stuff was coming up. She'd say, 'Hey, come look at this,' and show it to me with pride at what she'd managed to cough up.

"That, as gross as it was, was completely Rain. So let's not just talk about how strong and beautiful she was, because that was only part of what made up Rain."

* * *

An hour and countless recountings later I hugged Jessie's friend, Anna, as the attendees milled about the space.

Anna pulled back, tears in her eyes. "I still can't believe it. I just talked to her the other day. She sounded fine."

I nodded. "She fooled us all. I thought she was getting stronger."

"She said she was drinking this special tea and you guys were looking into other alternatives. I thought she'd be okay."

My throat tightened. "I'm so sorry. I know this is a shock. She wouldn't let me call any of you when she went into the hospital. She didn't want anyone to see her. She didn't want you to worry. We were lucky to get her home again. She was drinking the Essiac tea and we were looking at other alternatives for when she got stronger."

Anna had lots of company in her grief. A young crowd filled those two viewing rooms that day. Word had spread beyond the ones we'd called. They were strong and healthy and fearless. It was hard for them to accept that one of their own had fallen.

* * *

A day or two later I was returning from an errand as I turned into our subdivision. A figure on a bicycle approached, coming from the direction of our house. As the figure drew nearer I slowed the car. It was Jessie's friend, Jack.

I rolled down the window and stopped beside him, sorrow and regret filling me at the pained look on his face. He said, "I was just coming from your house. I couldn't believe it when I heard. I'm so sorry."

I nodded. "Thank you, Jack. Look, I'm sorry I didn't let you see her that night."

He shrugged. "It's okay. I'm really sorry about before."

Again, I nodded. "She was really happy that you'd come back into her life."

"I'm glad that I at least got to make things right with her, you know?"

"Yeah."

"I should let you go. Again, I'm so sorry."

Tears stung my eyes. "Me, too."

* * *

I took one more week off from work. I had plenty of donated time in my vacation bank, but I wasn't going to feel any better at home, with so many memories pressing all around me. The lightheartedness with which the conversation with Rosalea had gifted me waned, though I felt intermittent sparks of it from time to time. Once, I sang at work and someone commented to me that I seemed happy. I was at times, but so many others found me slipping into an empty office where I could quietly fall to pieces in private.

At home, I'd sometimes sit on Jessie's bed while Newt and Lindsey were busy elsewhere. The stillness of the house would blanket me and I'd let myself miss her. I felt it would help to let the grief flow rather than bottle it up and let it fester. I wanted my kids to know it was okay for them to grieve as well, so I didn't try to hide it. My preference, though, was to grieve in private.

In those early days I learned my private grieving could happen pretty easily in public, too, though. If I didn't make eye contact or draw attention to my tears by wiping them away, I could cry around others in elevators, in hallways, or while grocery shopping without them noticing. People tend to keep to themselves in those scenarios. Other times, I just didn't care if they noticed.

Before she was discharged from the hospital, Jessie had asked me to buy her new underwear, since she'd be home in her own clothes and she'd want to be comfortable.

"All I have are thongs," she'd said.

I'd taken it as a good sign that she was more and more okay with me leaving her alone at the hospital for short periods. I'd hit Target and picked up the new panties, along with a few other items she'd need at home.

She never wore the panties and one day I grabbed them, still in the bag. It made me sad to have them around and they were in perfect condition to be restocked. As I headed into the store, I couldn't hold back the grief, though. I suppose it was one of those moments I just didn't care.

I kept on my sunglasses, but they didn't hide the fact that I was crying. I handed the girl behind the customer service counter the bag with the receipt. "I don't need these."

"Are you okay?"

I shook my head, barely able to speak. I couldn't be further away from okay. "No."

She didn't ask me anything else as she completed my return.

I never knew when the grief would hit like that. I learned to carry moisturizer in my purse to dab under my eyes where the salt from my tears had a particularly detrimental effect. Sometimes it was unbearable, others less so. The quiet times were the worst. Any time I was alone, especially when I was driving in the car, turned into a crying fest. On the streets and interstates around Atlanta, Georgia, I pulled my anonymity around me like a shield, remained focused on the road and wept.

Once I opened a drawer in the kitchen and found all these packets of au jus seasoning. It was a favorite of Jessie's and I'd stocked it specifically for her. The grief drove me to my knees that time.

As the days passed it did get easier, though over a long time, and even now I still have those moments that have me in fetal position on the floor. I suppose it will always be this way. I kept with me the advice given in an online forum for parents of children with cancer. One mother had asked how she could keep from falling to pieces.

Another responded, "You don't. You fall to pieces when you need to and then you pick yourself up and move on."

I do have many happy memories of Jessie, though, and I feel her with me often. I do my best to focus on the happier memories.

Meanwhile, Newt and Lindsey carried on. For one of her class assignments, Lauren had been asked to share her most valued possession.

"I think I'll take my shoes," she'd said. She had a pair she really liked that were hanging upside down from her ceiling in an artsy kind of way.

"That would be nice," I said.

But a couple of days later she said, "I've changed my mind. I think I'll share the cryo-babies."

Jessie had willed her cryopreserved embryos to Lauren. I was in the process of transferring the paperwork at the clinic. Afterwards, I asked Lauren, "So, how did it go at school?"

Newt had taken a copy of Jessie's will and told the story of her sister and the embryos. She inhaled slowly. "I didn't know I'd get emotional talking about it."

"I know, honey, it can be hard. What did everyone say?"

"They didn't say anything. They just kind of stared." She shrugged. "And then the teacher gave me extra credit for having the most unusual possession."

I couldn't help smiling over that.

CHAPTER SIXTEEN

No Goodbyes

HARTSFIELD INTERNATIONAL AIRPORT was busy as usual on July 18, 2006, as I pulled to the passenger drop-off curb. Larry hadn't been able to take Rain to Costa Rica, but he was making good on his promise to take Lauren and Lindsey. I'd insisted on driving them all to the airport in an effort to spend every last moment with my kids.

"Here," I handed Lindsey their backpack from the back of my minivan as Larry grabbed their rolling bag. "You stay close to your sister and Dad, okay?"

"Of course I will." They threw the backpack on and then hugged me. "Will you be okay?"

"Me?" I smiled. "Of course."

"You can get some writing done," Newt said as she in turn hugged me.

"Absolutely."

I'd tried to write, truly I had, but I'd been desperate for a normal existence since Rain's passing. We hadn't had normal in so long and I owed it to my kids to give them whatever normalcy we could muster. Besides, the writing took so much additional energy on top of everything else and I was running on empty most of the time.

"I love you," I said to my kids, and then before I got weepy-eyed, I waved them off and then headed for home.

When I arrived, the quiet of the house surrounded me. I climbed the stairs to Jessie's room and sat on her bed. I tried not to let myself do this too often, but that day I allowed myself to sit in the stillness and miss her. Maybe if I let myself get it all out of my system at the start, the rest of the week would go easier.

I filled the week with other activities, cleaning the house, organizing my drawers, anything but writing. The camel dream haunted me, but I still felt so raw. I couldn't even bring myself to turn on Alphie.

And then, after all the months of waiting, I dreamed of Rain. She sat at the foot of my bed and she wasn't happy with me. I awoke with the gnawing feeling it was because I wasn't writing her story.

* * *

My mom arrived for a visit a couple of days before my kids returned. We enjoyed some quiet time while I got ready to attend the Romance Writers of America's national conference later that week. I'd taken the fact that the conference was being held in Atlanta as a sign that it was time for me to reenter the writing world.

The kids arrived home, and Mom and Lindsey joined me at the conference's Literacy Autographing. Since I'd had no new releases in 2006 and nothing in the works as far as future releases, I wasn't participating in the signing. We walked the rows of the ballroom full of hundreds of romance authors, and Mom and I loaded up on books. The following day I attended workshops and networked.

I felt like I was doing well with my goal of maintaining a state of normalcy as I reacquainted myself with the ever-changing publishing industry. I relaxed a little and joined my editor, Wanda, and some of her other authors at a dinner. I managed small talk with the authors, most of whom I'd never met.

And then the woman sitting across from me asked the most innocent of questions. "So, how many children do you have?"

I hesitated. "I have...two children."

Guilt niggled at me. I felt like I was somehow betraying Jessie, but I couldn't bring myself to include her in my head count at this point. I didn't really know these people. What if they asked about my third child? How would I explain without making the conversation uncomfortable?

The next day I attended a party for Blaze, the line with which I'd published my books to date. It was a festive affair, open to the public. I stood amongst the crowd of Harlequin editors, authors and readers, enjoying the moment.

An author friend I knew from online smiled and greeted me as she moved to my side in the crowd. "Dorene, how are you?"

I greeted her in return. "I'm well. I'm glad the conference was in Atlanta this year. I kind of had to come."

"That's right, you're local."

"Yes." We chatted about the conference and then she asked, "So, how is your daughter?"

I stared at her, caught completely off guard. I'd forgotten she knew my daughter had been sick. Most of the people I knew who were attending were well aware of what had happened with Jessie. I hadn't prepared myself for this particular scenario. Momentarily speechless, I shook my head.

She frowned.

I inhaled slowly. "She passed in April."

Tears filled the woman's eyes. There, in the middle of the Harlequin Blaze party, she wept. I touched her arm, unsure what to say to comfort her. "I'm...sorry."

"No, I'm sorry." She shook her head.

"It's okay." I stood with her a moment longer while she pulled herself together.

That evening found me in a crowded ballroom, full of festive lights and music. It was the annual Harlequin party. I stood chatting with my editor, my agent, Annelise Robey with the Jane Rotrosen Agency, and another author.

Again, came the same awkward question. The author asked, "How many children do you have?"

I glanced at my editor and answered, "Two."

"And what are they doing tonight?" the author asked.

"They're ordering room service and watching on demand movies. They're at the hotel with me."

"So you live in the area, but you're all staying downtown for the conference?"

"Yes," I said. "It's a treat for them and I like having them close."

The conversation continued and I relaxed again and let my guard down. We talked about writing, the industry and then circled back to my kids at some point. Out of sheer habit I made a passing reference to my three children.

The other author frowned. "I thought you had two kids. Where is your third one?"

I stared at her tongue-tied as a vision of my other author friend bursting into tears during the Blaze party floated through my mind. I glanced at my agent and then back at the woman. "I have no idea how to answer that."

Annelise slipped her arm around my shoulders and explained my very odd response to the author. The woman burst into tears, and I realized that we all have trauma in our lives and we all deal with it to the best of our abilities, often suppressing it to carry on with our daily routines. Sometimes just the mention of another's traumatic experience can trigger the grief we fight to suppress.

My friends helped me to keep these experiences in perspective. Patti Henry told me of another friend who'd lost a child.

"When people asked how many children she had, she'd say she had two here with her and one in heaven," she said.

I adapted this to something more palatable to Rain and learned to use it with new friends, because, inevitably, I'd mention Jessie. She'd been a part of my life for nineteen years and she'd be alive in my memories forever.

* * *

September neared and I knew we had to plan a memorial for Jessie's birthday, especially since Phoenix had been in boot camp when she passed and had missed the first memorial service.

"I've ordered the model of a Viking ship, but we still need to figure out where," I said to Lauren. "I've been asking her, but she hasn't answered. Maybe we should hold it in the Gulf of Mexico."

Lauren crinkled her nose. "She hated the beach."

I smiled. "I know; there's sand on the beach. But we have to plan something and Destin is a central location. It works logistically for the people on her guest list and we can see my family there."

"I suppose you're right."

And so we planned Rain's Viking burial to take place on her first birthday after her passing.

* * *

My head pounded and I ached all over as I drove my minivan full of kids to Destin, Florida. Lindsey rode down with Larry, but Lauren and I had brought Cytney and Phoenix with us. The week before our trip I'd hit an all-time emotional low as Jessie's first birthday since her passing had neared. As a result, I'd come down with the worst case of the flu I'd ever had before or since.

The only bright spot was that I'd finally heard from Jessie. My dear friend Kimberly Brock, another author friend who'd met Jessie on only one occasion, had emailed me.

I had a dream and I don't know what it means, but I knew I needed to tell you about it. I saw Jessie. She had braids, like an Indian princess and she was swimming in a lake. Does that mean anything to you?

I'd smiled and answered immediately, thanking Jessie as I did so. Dreams had played such an important role in this journey so far. Of course, this is where I'd find my answer.

Yes, that's Jessie telling me where she wants her ashes.

Kim's response made me laugh. *Don't freak me out or anything.*

We determined the lake in her dream was somewhere southwest of Seattle, in an area where Kim had once visited. She didn't know the exact lake but was sure that was the area.

I was miserable as we headed to Florida for Jessie's birthday, but at least I now had a plan for the anniversary of her passing. We'd spend her birthday with people she loved and who loved her. Then in the spring, Lindsey, Lauren and I would take some of Rain's ashes and find that lake near Seattle.

* * *

I can't say how many times in my life I'd made the trip from Atlanta to Destin, but I can say I was never happier to finish that drive than on that day when we arrived at the Rum Boogie

Bungalow, the beach house I'd rented for Jessie's birthday memorial. We entered the house and followed the first steps down into the in-law suite, before ascending to the next floor with the second kitchen, bedrooms and wrap-around decks. As we explored room after room, balcony after balcony and deck after deck, I forgot briefly about my pounding head and aching body.

"It just keeps going," Newt said as we climbed the final stairs to the owner's suite at the top. The room stretched before us with its open floor plan, hot tub and private balcony overlooking the pool below.

"She might not have liked the beach, but she would have liked it here." I smiled as I stepped out onto the balcony and the salt-scented breeze brushed by me.

We filled the house with her friends and some of my family stopped by. The afternoon before her "Viking" memorial, I sat on one of the decks. Lauren had prepared parchment paper on which we'd each write notes to Jessie.

As I filled the page with all of the words I'd left unsaid between us, I soaked up the sun, feeling better than on the drive down. "Jess, we're going to do our best to honor your wishes."

Prior to her original memorial, Maureen and Lauren had decorated green, blue, yellow, pink and other jewel-toned glass bottles with ribbons, feathers, shells and other items. During the ash ceremony we wanted everyone to have a little of Jessie's ashes to pour into the model of the Viking ship along with our letters.

A few days before, while we were still at home getting ready for the trip, I'd been slightly uneasy over the prospect of filling the bottles that we'd transport with us. As usual, Lauren was there to help me through it.

"Let's go out back," I said as Lindsey was busy in their room. The thought of opening the box of Jessie's ashes had me a little spooked, and I thought maybe it would be better to keep it away from my youngest child.

"I'll get the bottles," Newt said as she headed to retrieve the basket of corked bottles.

We spread newspaper over the grass and then I turned over the box of ashes and removed the screw holding the bottom sliding panel in place. I opened the box and peered inside. "They're in a plastic bag."

I'm not sure what I'd expected, but I was surprised by the bag. Though it was made of thick plastic, it seemed extraordinarily ordinary for its purpose. I pulled the bag from the wooden box. It was heavy. A metal tag identified the remains with Jessie's name and date of passing. I removed it and set it carefully aside, along with the rubber band holding the bag closed.

I held my breath as I gazed at the coarse bits of white, gray and black. The consistency of the ashes ranged from large granules to a fine powder. My mind had difficulty comprehending that this was all that was left of Rain. My stomach tightened, but I pushed aside my apprehension and I glanced at Newt, intent by my side.

"We need something to scoop it out with and maybe a funnel," I said. I rubbed a corner of the plastic bag. It was actually very practical and there was no reason we couldn't also be practical in our filling of the bottles.

"I know what to get," I said as I set down the bag and then headed toward the house.

A few minutes later I returned with a small plastic shovel from the beach bag and a plastic cone-shaped cup lid with a hole for a straw. It made a perfect funnel.

Newt had already managed to pour some of the ashes directly from the plastic bag into one of the small-necked bottles. I admired how she did so without any squeamishness. She shook a little ash off of her hand onto the newspaper.

"Here, let's try this." I knelt beside her and placed the makeshift funnel over the opening of one of the bottles.

We took turns holding the funnel and pouring small shovelfuls into the colorful containers, going slowly to let the contents filter down without spilling over the top. With a little practice, I was able to set aside the shovel and pour directly from the bag. It took a little time, but we managed to get them all partially filled and we'd brought the bottles of ash with us to Destin.

Lauren stepped onto the deck, bringing my thoughts back to the present. The plan was to launch the little Viking ship at sunset that day. Afterwards, we'd feast on all of Jessie's favorite foods, here at the beach house.

"Everyone is writing their notes," Lauren said.

I nodded. "We can each share a memory, then put in our notes and pour the ashes into the model of the Viking ship before we light it on fire."

"That sounds nice," she said. "And we'll be able to do it at sunset?"

"Yes, we're to be at the dock at dusk."

* * *

Dressed in varying combinations of black and white, our small party reached the dock as the sun hung low in the sky. I glanced at it in trepidation. "We aren't going to have much time."

The boat pitched as the young captain, Jeff, assisted us all onboard. This might not be where or how Jessie had wanted her burial, but it was as close to a Viking burial—which I'd learned were brutal, often sending a live spouse to burn with the departed—as we could get. As we plowed toward the darkening horizon I turned to the solemn faces of our party.

"I don't think we're going to have much time to each share a memory like we'd hoped. So, let's just load it up and get ready."

The wind whipped around us as the sun descended lower in the sky and the boat rocked on the choppy water. Hurriedly, each member of the memorial party stepped forward and emptied ashes from his or her jewel-colored bottle into the little wooden ship. As we stuffed the last of the letters in with the ashes, Jeff cut the engine.

I stared at the bright glow of the sun as we bobbed, the surf rocking us erratically. I turned to our captain. "How will we do this?"

He gestured toward an opening at the back of the boat, facing the brilliant sunset.

I stared at the waves crashing against the boat and pointed at the wooden model. "You know we're going to light that on fire."

He nodded. "I understand. You can hold it out the back, light it, and then set it in the water."

"But what will keep it from crashing back into your boat? I'd hate to set your boat on fire."

He handed me a long metal pole. "You'll push it away with this."

"Okay." I took the pole, though it did little to ease my concern over the choppy waters.

Phoenix and Josh, another of Rain's friends, took over the launching of the miniature boat. I'd brought lighter fluid, but thought better of using it since it was a wooden boat stuffed full of paper and ashes. Before I could mention this, though, the boys hosed the model down with the lighter fluid. Then, as Josh held it out of the opening over the rough water, Phoenix lit his lighter. The four-inch flame had my heart pounding. He held the flame to the little wooden ship and it erupted like a fireball, while Josh still held it.

In a panic, I shoved forward with the pole. Before all of our astonished gazes the little ship disappeared below the water's surface, the flame extinguishing as the tiny mast submerged. A moment of stunned silence blanketed us, and then Josh turned to me, his eyes wide. "You sank it."

As the wind whipped around me, I could feel Jessie's laughter and I shrugged. I felt horribly disappointed, but I couldn't do anything about it now.

"You still accomplished what you wanted," Jeff said.

I nodded as the sun's last rays dipped below the horizon.

"Yes." I sighed. "And I didn't light your boat on fire."

* * *

Fall melted into winter, which brought us again to spring and the trip we'd planned in response to Kim's dream of Jessie swimming in a lake. The kids and I had never been as far west as Seattle. Our flight was delayed and we ran to catch our connecting flight from Denver. After arriving in Seattle, we drove for another two and a half hours southwest, along a secluded track of road with wide swatches of evergreens on both sides, to a small resort. We gave ourselves three days to search all the lakes in the area.

We ruled out several lakes in the first two days, but on the third day, I was hopeful when we set out for our last exploratory drive. We drove through mountainous terrain with trees crowding in on all sides. The lake came into sight as we rounded a bend, its blue surface sparkling in the afternoon sun.

Goose flesh rippled over me from head to toe. I smiled at Lauren in the passenger seat of our rental car. This was the response for which I'd been waiting.

"That's it. I just had a whoosh." I held my arm out to her. "See the goose bumps."

187

"It looks big," she said, her smile matching mine. We'd travelled nearly twenty-seven-hundred miles across country to find this lake.

"How do we get there?" Lindsey asked from the back.

"I don't know." I glanced at the map as I maneuvered along the shaded road. "I think this way will get us closer."

We turned onto a side road and drove through a subdivision with houses bordering the lake. Its blue surface sparkled in the sunlight and stretched to the horizon.

"It *is* big," Lindsey said.

"Look at the mountains in the distance." I took another turn to keep us close to the shoreline.

Lauren grabbed the map. She pointed. "Go this way, Mom. We need to find some place more private. This is too populated."

I followed her directions as the road changed from paved to gravel and then dirt and then the dirt road ended. "What now?" I asked. "We're not close enough to the lake. Maybe I should turn back and look for another way."

"No, Mom, keep going," Newt urged. "There's still a path."

We bumped along the path as it grew more and more narrow. Laughter bubbled up inside me. "Oh, my God, we're off roading in our rental car."

We drove as far as we could and then I parked under a grove of trees. The Northwest grew some amazing trees. We left the car and continued the rest of the way on foot, down a craggy incline to a sandy area below, with the lake spread in all its majesty just beyond the beach.

Lauren handed me the small glass bottle that held Jessie's ashes. "You do it."

I turned toward the mountains beyond the far shore, facing a valley between two of the snow-capped peaks. "Well, my Jess, I hope this is where you meant. It feels right. I'm sorry about the whole Viking burial thing, but we did our best. I hope you at least found it amusing. I love you, honey. I always will."

A bird cawed in the distance. A soft breeze curled around me as I emptied the small bottle into the clear water where the current ran, carrying the water toward the mountains on the far side of the lake.

"Here, I'll rinse it." Newt dipped the empty bottle under the current.

We stayed a short while longer, letting the peace of the area soak into us. It was one of the most beautiful places I've ever been. Lauren took pictures with a disposable camera, which we, unfortunately, left in the rental car. I'll always remember that lake, though, with the reflection of the mountains and sky rippling across its surface and the comforting peace that enveloped me as I stood on its shore.

*　*　*

I think if anyone were to ask me if I said goodbye to Jessie that day, I'd have to say no. Why say goodbye when she is still with me? I feel her around me often. I talk to her and feel her responses. She's my inside connection to the other side. Though I have others, just as we all do, my connection with her is stronger. I know she's okay.

She's gone home.

I know she has been patiently waiting for me to write her story—our story. We were all affected in more ways than I could ever recount in these pages, not only by her passing, but by her life, as well. So, this story belongs to all of us who knew and loved her.

My writing came back to me slowly. I started the original draft of this book years ago, but though the number of pages here may be short, the telling of this story was a long and difficult process for me. I wrote as much as I could, when I could. When I couldn't bring myself to work on this project, and there were long stretches of time when I could not, I worked on my fiction writing. I returned briefly to Harlequin and wrote two more romance novels for their Superromance line.

At some point during that time I dreamed again of Rain. She rose from the water, the droplets sparkling off her as she stood before me.

"I'm poor," she said.

I awoke feeling uneasy. What was she telling me? I interpreted that particular dream to say that she was lacking attention from me, that she needed me to finish her story. So I again put aside my fiction writing to pull this project off the back burner. I didn't feel I could move forward in other areas of my writing until completing this project.

I hope the next time I dream of Jessie she'll be more approving. I hope she's happy with the way this memoir has unfolded. I've asked her for her input all along the way. I think I've gotten it right. If my only purpose in writing this was for my own cathartic process, then I have accomplished that. I have healed in many ways. Anything beyond that would be icing on the cake.

Friends have asked how I've been able to move on after such a loss. I still feel it, no doubt, and when the grief takes hold, I let myself fall to pieces as needed, but then I pick myself up and carry on. I have two more beautiful children who mean the world to me and will maybe have my grandbabies one day. I'm being patient for now, since it'll be some time before Lauren or Lindsey are ready for children of their own. I'm also perfectly okay with not having grandchildren. I only want my children to be happy.

But you never know what the future will bring. We still have Jessie's cryopreserved embryos to consider. Every year I get the bill on the storage for them and I ask Lauren what we should do with them and though Rain left them to her, she has so far left that decision up to me.

Every year I pay the storage. After all, they're a part of Jessie we still have. They're a symbol of hope for me, reminding me of the laughter we found even during the most difficult days. We have come through the darkness to a brighter place and we are changed because of this experience. We have found strength and a new perspective, but most of all, we have found healing and so much love in sharing our memories of passing Rain.

DORENE GRAHAM BIO

As a child, Dorene carried around Little Golden Books and pretended to read them to her younger siblings. She was initially struck by the writing muse at the tender age of nine, when she stayed up past her bedtime for the first time ever to finish a short story. That attempt resulted in her teacher reading her work aloud to the class, then submitting her story to Highlights magazine. Unfortunately, Dorene took the magazine's request to shorten the story as a flat rejection.

Over the years she followed the muse from time to time, but didn't get serious about writing until after the birth of her third child. Even then it took about five years of juggling husband, children, nonprofit work, and her writing before she finally mastered the art of rejection and landed her first sale in September 2001. Over the following twelve years she published six Blazes and two Superromances with Harlequin. Then in 2019, she published her memoir, Passing Rain.

Currently, she resides in Jonesboro, Georgia, a suburb of metro-Atlanta. Now in 2023, she finds herself in the happy position of being able to pursue her writing full time. When not on the lake kayaking, or hanging with family and friends, you'll find her exploring her creative nature, and, of course, writing.

Please drop by www.dorenegraham.com for more information.

Passing Rain   Dorene Buckley Graham

Made in the USA
Monee, IL
07 June 2023